Urgent Advice
from Your Catholic Grandpa

Robert A. Young

URGENT ADVICE FROM YOUR CATHOLIC GRANDPA

iUniverse books may be ordered through booksellers or by contacting:

iUniverse
1663 Liberty Drive
Bloomington, IN 47403
www.iuniverse.com
1-800-Authors (1-800-288-4677)

Because of the dynamic nature of the Internet, any web addresses or links contained in this book may have changed since publication and may no longer be valid. The views expressed in this work are solely those of the author and do not necessarily reflect the views of the publisher, and the publisher hereby disclaims any responsibility for them.

ISBN: 978-1-5320-1890-9 (sc)
ISBN: 978-1-5320-1889-3 (e)

Library of Congress Control Number: 2017903723

Print information available on the last page.

iUniverse rev. date: 03/27/2017

Table of Contents

Dedication

This book is dedicated to my grandchildren, current and future: Justin, Katie, Zacchaeus, Maximilian, Kateri, Therese, Miguel, Philomena, Marguerite, Felicity, Colton, Dakota, Nicholas, Theresa, Luke, Matthew, Emma, James, Averie, Elise, Christopher, Trinity, Grace, Mary, Justice, Faith, Colby, Isabelle, Simon, and ....

May these gifts from God our Father reflect brightly the light of Truth and the fire of Love.

Photo by SMO Photo

Acknowledgements

Thanks to every member of my family who helped me extensively in creating this book: Mary, Christie, Angela, Nichole, Heidi, Rob, Ryan, Marianne, Russell, and Heather. The final work was substantially different than the initial draft, thanks to their persistence and loving involvement.

Thanks to Glenda Chaison for reading an early draft of the book and suggesting improvements and giving me encouragement to continue.

Thanks to AnnMarie Kennedy for her creativity guidance.

Thanks to my friend, William (Bill) Robbins, who reviewed the book and validated my comments on Judaism.

Thanks to Father Justin Cinnante and Father Joseph Gill. Their critiques and suggestions were essential to the integrity of the content.

And finally, thanks to the Holy Spirit for guiding the entire effort to lead us all to a better relationship with Truth!

Why Did I Write This Book?

I wrote this book because I am dying. Now don't panic. I have no specific news in that regard. I am dying because I will not live forever. I am seventy-three years old and in the twilight of my life. You are dying also, but you will likely live for many more years.

My desire is to convey the important things I have learned over the last seventy-three years so that you will have a joy-filled life in this world and in the next.

The most important aspect of this book relates to the **decisions** you will make in the future and my recommendations about those decisions.

But to make sound decisions, one has to have a **decision-making framework**. A faithful, informed Catholic has that framework and can answer the following questions:

- Is there a God?
- Is that God Catholic?
- Is the Bible relevant?
- How do I get real-time guidance?
- What is my role in the spiritual war?

Many of you reading this book are already deeply immersed into the Catholic faith and can answer those questions. But for those who are not, the appendix of this book describes the basics of Catholicism, which you might find helpful.

Now before you continue reading this book, ask yourself the question. "<u>Why</u> am I reading this book?"

Let me reveal now one of the main assertions made in this book: **There are no accidents!** After you read this book, you will understand why God brought it to you.

The Primal Decision

Dear grandchildren, God gives each of us two gifts: <u>time</u> and <u>free will</u>. We don't know how much time we have here on earth. But, during our time here, our free will is what makes us unique as persons. We can ***decide***. During our lifetime we will make thousands upon thousands of decisions.

We will become the sum total of all those decisions we make. Our body will be gone after we die. We are told that we will have a resurrected body, but we don't know exactly what that will be like. So in the end, that which makes us unique will be the sum total of our decisions we make in this life.

My goal in this book is to convey <u>urgent advice</u> to you about how you should make those decisions.

There are small decisions, and there are huge decisions. A small decision might be, "Will I have oatmeal for breakfast, or will I have a fried egg for breakfast?" A big decision will be something like, "Should I marry this boy or should I marry this girl?"

The <u>primal decision</u>, the most fundamental decision, is the decision that you make in relation to God. Do you want to follow <u>God's will</u>? Or do you want to follow <u>your own will</u>?

This primal decision will determine your entire future, both in this life, and in the eternal life thereafter. It is a very basic question. Do you want to live in Heaven? Or do you want to live in Hell?

The problem people have today is that they often never make a conscious decision. Many of them have chosen Hell, but are completely unaware that they have made that decision.

Generally speaking, if you have not made a <u>conscious</u> decision that you want to live in Heaven, you may have <u>subconsciously chosen Hell</u> by your lifestyle. <u>Upon death, that decision becomes final for eternity.</u>

I will share my own experience. I did make a decision very young that I wanted to live in Heaven. But to make that decision work, to make it operative, one has to commit 100% to be obedient to God's will. Until I was nearly fifty years old, my decision was that I would be 99.99% obedient to God's will. I was willing to be obedient to God's will, as long as He didn't tell me that I should travel to Africa and live with lepers the rest of my life. I knew I just couldn't handle that. Therefore I knew I could be obedient to God's will in most cases, **but I didn't trust God enough to be 100% committed**.

What changed my life was when I realized I could trust God. In my spiritual reading I came across the story of a visionary who had received a message from Jesus. In that message Jesus said, "If you commit to obey, I will give you peace and joy." After some prayer and reflection, I realized that one of two things would happen if I committed. Either He would not send me to Africa to take care of the lepers; or if He did, it would give me peace and joy. **Therefore, if I committing to obey, I couldn't lose either way.** Wow! That was a revelation! I didn't reach that point until I was almost fifty years old. So late one night, while lying in bed, I made the big commitment. **I said to God, "I will <u>obey</u> You, because I know that You will give me peace and joy if I do."**

The next morning when I woke up, I didn't realize it, but my life was about to change dramatically. It was as if I had been blind and now I could see. I had found the pearl of great value and was willing to sell everything to own it (Matthew 13:46). It was incredible. **Suddenly I <u>became aware</u> of God's presence in my life. Every moment of every**

day became an encounter with the living God who created me and sustains me, and who is constantly intervening in my life. I came to realize that in this life *"there are no accidents."* There are no coincidences. In other words, *everything that happens is orchestrated by our loving God and Father.* It was an astounding revelation.

I made the commitment to obey God 100% on November 24, 1991. Then on December 8, 1992, about one year later, I consecrated myself to Jesus through the Blessed Virgin Mary. This Marian Consecration was completed using the Saint Louis de Montfort 33-day course of preparation. The Lord led me to do this when I came to realize that the act of consecrating oneself to Jesus through Mary added another dimension to one's spiritual growth; it was like adding a booster rocket to my spiritual life.

I completed this consecration during an all-day meditation at the Miraculous Medal Chapel located at the Rue de Bac in Paris, France. At the end of the day there I bought a Miraculous Medal and have worn it around my neck every moment for the last twenty-five years.

Then in January of 1993 I met someone else who had consecrated himself to Mary: Saint Pope John Paul II. Wow! Unbelievable! About a year after I committed myself 100% to God, and to Jesus through the Blessed Virgin Mary, I was shaking hands with the Pope. Really? Really! It was undoubtedly Divine Providence. *There are no accidents.* What a gift from God! Unknown to me at the time was that the Pope was also consecrated in the same way and that his motto, inspired by Saint Louis de Monfort, was "Totus Tuus" in Latin, which means "Totally Yours" in English.

During the brief personal encounter with the Pope, I was moved by the Spirit to expose my Miraculous Medal on the outside of my clothing. The moment he noticed my medal, he turned and gave his secretary a signal. Moments later Pope John Paul II was handing the gift of a Rosary to me and another to my wife, Mary, which he then blessed.

Then just to top off this providential miraculous encounter with a living Saint, my wife asked the Pope to bless our family. He did! The photos which follow capture that moment.

Now why am I telling you all this? For one simple reason: I want you to have a miraculous experience with our living God before you are fifty years old and your life is more than half over. The exciting thing is that many of you may have already made this decision to commit. Thanks to your grandma primarily, and me to some extent, your parents have, for the most part, already made this decision to commit to God and to obey 100%. And they have passed their faith on to you.

This primal decision to commit 100% results in unlocking the power of God in our lives. As an example, my son, Ryan, and his wife, Elizabeth, have made this critical first commitment. One result of that decision is the miraculous formation of Camp Veritas, an amazing vehicle to effect spiritual conversions of both teenagers and adults. More information about this miracle camp can be found at **www.campveritas.org**.

The faith your parents have passed on to you is their greatest gift to you. This faith is their belief in a loving, involved God who participates actively in every moment of your life, and who wants what is best for you.

Before you continue reading this book, you need to <u>stop reading right now</u> and put this book down. Ask yourself the question: "Have I committed to obey God 100% the rest of my life? If I have not, why not? Don't I trust God?"

If you have made this primal decision, then continue reading and we will get into some of the details about how to make other decisions that will help you along your path to Heaven.

God is like our parents in many ways. Imagine if your parents said to you, "Six months from now during Christmas you are going to receive the most fantastic gift and it will be greater than something you could ever, ever, ever want or ask for." Would you question them? Or would you trust them and follow their advice during the next six months so that you would be able to receive the gift?

God is the same way. Jesus has promised us a reward which is

Heaven and which is described in the Bible as "Eye has not seen and ear has not heard what I have prepared for you who love Me" (1 Cor. 2:9). Jesus also says, "In my Father's house there are many dwelling places" (John 14:2).

So what is your decision? Are you willing to obey God 100% the rest of your life? Or do you want to negotiate this life using only your own skills and knowledge?

Your eternal life and your eternal happiness depend on that decision. And you don't know how much time you have. You might die tomorrow. If you make the wrong decision today it may be too late to change it a week from now.

That is why I consider the advice I give you as urgent. It is urgent, urgent, urgent, urgent! Don't mess around.

I especially want to say to you, my grandkids, "I love you. You are my flesh and blood. I want you to be with our loving family in Heaven for eternity. We are one in Spirit! Praise God!"

The Goal of Peace

It is all about peace.

I try to say the Rosary every morning. When I do, the intention is always the same. I say, "Blessed Mother, I offer this Rosary up for your intentions, especially for peace in the world which begins with peace in our hearts and peace in our families."

So what is this peace all about?

To be at peace is to know that you are doing God's will at that moment. Believe it or not, it is a very difficult thing to achieve. Why is that?

The reason peace is so difficult is that God placed us in a war zone. There is a war going on in the world. People are killing other people. People are hurting other people. People are fighting over things.

People will do anything to get more power. It is a dog-eat-dog world out there. And we have no choice but to live in that world. It is where God put us.

Even more challenging is that there is also a war zone <u>inside</u> us. Satan is extremely busy trying to keep us from doing God's will. Ordinarily he does this through **temptations**: we are tempted to do what is pleasurable; we are tempted to do things which build up a false self-image. The overriding temptation is to be "like God." *That is the <u>root of all sin</u>: we want to be God. That sin is called <u>pride</u>.*

So our critical <u>barometer</u> used to determine whether or not we are doing God's will is the <u>awareness of our level of peace</u>.

Our objective, our goal, is to rest in God's peace at every moment of every day. If we are in the state of peace, then we know that we are doing God's will. And it is only in that state that God's will can be achieved through us and the world can be changed. Jesus told us, "Apart from Me you can do nothing" (John 15:5). What He is telling us is that, no matter how hard we work, nothing of value can be accomplished unless we are at peace in the Lord.

So why is it so hard to achieve the state of peace? It is very simple. Satan, by his very nature, will engage us in **spiritual combat** and try to win. The way he wins is to get us focused on achieving worldly success. He wants us to focus on becoming rich and powerful. He wants us to focus on worldly goods which provide us pleasure. He wants to get us addicted to the things that distract us from doing what God would have us do.

One of Satan's key strategies is to get us focused on the <u>past</u> and to fill our minds with <u>guilt</u>. The other is to get us to focus on the <u>future</u> and fill our minds with <u>fear</u>. As long as our minds are filled with either guilt or fear, we are not in the <u>present moment</u>. Thus we are completely worthless in terms of being a vehicle for God's love to the world.

First, let us talk about how to deal with the thoughts Satan gives us about the **past** and the **guilt** that can come with that. To deal with that temptation, we must first understand and believe in the mercy of God. Once we confess our sins and are truly sorry for them, then they are gone. Jesus died on the cross for us to wipe away those sins. All we have to do is accept His gift to us. If we have failed to accept that gift, then we are limiting God's mercy. It is prideful to think that our sin is too great for God's mercy. And if we haven't learned how to forgive other people, then we cannot imagine how God could forgive us. That is why in the prayer called the "Our Father" *(i.e. the Lord's Prayer)* we ask God to "forgive us our trespasses as we forgive those who trespass against us." There are literally millions of people walking around today in the world who are unable to accept God's forgiveness because they themselves have not made the decision to forgive others. This is very sad. My advice: do NOT be a person who holds onto unforgiveness, whether the unforgiveness is directed towards others or inward towards yourself. Who have *you* failed to forgive?

Another tactic of Satan is to **discourage** us. **Ultimately, he wants us to despair—to give up!** You are in good company if you feel besieged by temptations and struggle to resist them. Saint Paul struggled mightily and asked the Lord for relief. *(Saint Paul was the primary apostle to the Gentiles immediately after the death of Jesus. While Saint Peter (an Apostle and the first Pope) focused on the Jews, Paul became the apostle who was sent to spread Christianity to the non-Jewish world (i.e. the Gentiles)).* If we read the Letters of Saint Paul, he very clearly states that even though he was trying to grow in perfection, he was severely tempted by one of his sinful habits. Then he tells us about his communication with God. He asked God to remove the temptation to that particular sin, and God said, "No. It is good for you to have that temptation. It keeps you humble and makes you realize that you can do nothing apart from Me." The exact quote from Saint Paul is as follows:

> 2 Cor. 12:7-10. ...Therefore, that I might not become too elated (for the revelations God gave to me), *a thorn in the flesh was given to me, an angel of Satan, to beat me,* to keep me from being too elated. *Three times I begged the Lord about this, that it might leave me,*

but *He said to me, "My grace is sufficient for you, for power is made perfect in weakness."* I will rather boast most gladly of my weaknesses, in order that the power of Christ may dwell with me. Therefore, I am content with weaknesses, insults, hardships, persecutions, and constraints, for the sake of Christ; *for when I am weak, then I am strong.*

So what happens is that Satan gets us focused on our weaknesses. When we realize how weak we are, we get discouraged. This gets us to *focus on the past* which is not where God wants us to be. So how do we deal with this? *The solution is to realize that once we sin, we ask God for forgiveness and we accept it. We commit to try to do better in the future and <u>ask God for His help</u> in becoming the person He wants us to be. Then we move on and move into the presence of Jesus in the current moment.*

Now let's talk about *fear* of the *future*. We all have fears of bad things that might happen to us in the future. We succumb to that temptation. All you need to do is watch the evening news on television and you will realize that the whole thrust of the news is to make you afraid. That is how they keep our attention. Fear is a strong motivating factor. Every news program shows us how other people are getting hurt. The implication is that we will be hurt if we are not fearful and take appropriate action to protect ourselves. Thus our thoughts and minds get directed to the future and we are not available to God in the present to do what He wants us to do. My advice: be aware of how fear is affecting your life! What are your five greatest fears?

So what about the future? How do we deal with the fear of the future?

It is very simple. It is simple but extremely difficult to do. *The way we deal with fear is to firmly believe that God is our Father, and that our Father has our best interests in mind.* Furthermore since our Father is God, there is nothing that is going to come to us in our life that is not from God! In other words, *<u>there are no accidents</u>. God can only give us what is good for us!* Wow!

This is one of the most difficult concepts for us to accept. This difficulty is the result of our Original Sin. Our Original Sin, which is the weakened state into which we are born, causes us to believe that <u>we cannot trust God</u>. Satan will whisper that lie in our ear constantly in order to reinforce that perception. <u>Our entire life is the process of re-education whereby we have to learn, over time, that we can trust God 100%!</u> He is looking out for us and can do nothing that is not in our best interest. Let me say it in another way without using two negatives. God can only give us what is good for our Eternal happiness. *(Note: To better understand the phrase "there are no accidents," I strongly recommend you read the short spiritual classic entitled **Trustful Surrender to Divine Providence** by Father Jean Baptiste Saint-Jure and Blessed Claude De La Colombiere.)*

Here I would like to interject a story told to me recently by a man who ten years ago was told that he only had six months to live. His name is Arthur (Artie) Boyle who lives near Boston. It turns out he was miraculously healed from inoperable cancer and attributes his healing to Jesus Christ through the intercession of the Blessed Virgin Mary.

Artie tells the following story at the beginning of his testimony.

> There was a wise farmer who lived in a small village. His neighbors considered him rich because he owned a horse. The horse did his field work for him.
>
> Then one day the horse disappeared. His neighbors gathered around and said, "It is a terrible thing that your horse disappeared."
>
> The farmer responded, "It could be good; it could be bad. Who knows?"
>
> Several days later, the farmer's horse reappeared and brought with him several other horses, one for each family in the small village. The villagers again addressed the farmer, "This is fantastic!"

The farmer responded, "It could be good; it could be bad. Who knows?"

The farmer then proceeded to train his horse and taught his 18-year-old son to ride it. The son happened to fall off the horse and break his leg. The villagers said to the farmer, "This is very bad. Aren't you upset with the turn of events? What are you going to do?"

Again, the farmer responded, "It could be good; it could be bad. Who knows?"

A week later the army came through town and forced every young able-bodied man to join them and go off to war. The army could not take the farmer's son because he had the broken leg. The villagers observed the situation and congratulated the farmer, "Wow! You must really be happy with what happened."

The farmer responded with <u>peace</u> in his voice, "It could be good; it could be bad. <u>Who knows</u>?"

So what is the point of the story? The story shows how God works in our lives. He has a plan for each of us, and His plan is beyond our comprehension. We are incapable of determining if events that happen in our life are good or bad. ***I would go beyond that and assert that <u>everything</u> that happens in our lives is <u>good</u>!***

In Artie's case he was told that he had inoperable cancer and only six months to live. Everyone said to him, "That is really bad." Ten years later, after Artie was healed ***<u>spiritually</u> and then physically***, he asserts that his death sentence was the best thing that ever happened to him and his family.

God had a plan for Artie; and ***He has a plan for you***. Everything that has happened to you and that is happening to you is an attempt by God to lead you to fulfill His plan for you in this life, so that you can be with Him in the next. Once you align your will to His, you can never again say, "Something bad happened to me." Rather, you will say, *"It could be good; it could be bad. Who knows?"* Or better yet, *"What happened to me is a gift from God's Providence, and therefore it has to be good!"*

So how do we stay in the present moment, which is where God wants us to be? Again, that is very simple. *We have to maintain a state of constant prayer.* Now constant prayer doesn't mean that for 24 hours a day 7 days a week we must be praying the Hail Mary or the Our Father. What it means is that we need to try to *be aware of God's presence every moment* we are awake. It is great if we can maintain a constant interchange with God. Many of you young people have that ability. You maintain a constant texting relationship with some of your friends. It is like that with God. We need to keep the chatter going constantly. God thank You for this; God thank You for that; God help me with this; God help me with that; God please help that person who is suffering; and so forth.

One final comment about peace. Peace and pain can exist at the same time. In fact that is very likely the norm. When Jesus had the conversation with His Father in the Garden of Gethsemane, *He made the decision* to accept His destiny, which He knew was going to be a horrible death. *He came to peace with that decision* (Matthew 26:36-46). Now obviously He was in excruciating mental and emotional pain as He made that decision. Then He experienced severe physical pain for many hours during His Passion until He was crucified and died. *But He had peace of mind; He knew He was doing His Father's will.*

So that is what peace is all about. Stay out of the past; stay out of the future. <u>Remain in the present</u> resting in our Lord Jesus Christ and allowing our Father to effect His will through us.

Spiritual Communication and Navigation (Prayer)

Before we venture into discussing additional decisions you need to make beyond the primal decision, let us discuss in more detail the way we stay in communication with God and allow Him to help us navigate the road to Eternal happiness. In other words, let us talk more about prayer.

The most important thing to know about God is that He is ***present*** to you at every moment of your life, day and night! Let me repeat that. God is constantly involved in your life and hears every word you say and knows every thought you think! Yes, I know. That is a little scary.

Can we talk to the person of God? YES! Of course. Speaking to God is called prayer. But why doesn't He talk back to us? He does! But most of the time He does not speak aloud in words. He speaks in other ways which I will address in more detail later. A person who is trying to make the proper decisions on the path to Heaven attempts to maintain an ongoing communication with God throughout the day.

I will share with you the way I interact with God. It is not the perfect way, nor is it necessarily the best way, but it is how I try to maintain open communication with God at this time of my life. Each person has to develop his own approach.

Everything starts the first moment I awake in the morning. I say to God, "Father God, Lord, please give me the grace to do Your will today. And please give me the wisdom to know Your will." I will also repeat this prayer at random moments of the day, especially when I have to make some decision about how to spend my time.

Next I spend thirty minutes doing physical exercise. During that thirty minutes I say the Rosary and meditate on the life of Jesus. I consider prayer in this context a form of spiritual exercise. Thus, I am strengthening both my body and my spirit. Appendix VII lists the 20 Mysteries of the Rosary and the associated meditations I use.

At this stage of my life I have the time and opportunity to attend daily ***Mass***. Wow! What a great gift from God! Prior to Mass, my community says the ***Divine Office***, which is also called the ***Liturgy of the Hours. The Mass and the Divine Office together represent the official _public_ prayer life of the Catholic Church.***

The Mass, which is also called the Eucharistic Sacrifice or the Eucharistic Meal, is an incredible prayer. This prayer is based on the meal Jesus had with His Apostles the day before His crucifixion. It has evolved over time, under the direction of the Church leadership, to allow the community of believers to interact with God, the Angels, and the Saints in Heaven in a glorious meal whereby we give thanksgiving to God the Father for all His gifts and *join* the crucified Jesus to *__offer ourselves__* to the Father as a living sacrificial gift.

__The Mass has two major parts: the Liturgy of the __Word__ and the Liturgy of the __Eucharist__. The word "liturgy" means "work." The Liturgy of the Word provides spiritual food for our mind. The Liturgy of the Eucharist provides spiritual food for our heart.__

The Liturgy of the Word includes readings from the Bible along with other prayers. This is preceded by a prayer of repentance whereby we tell God we are sorry for our thoughts, words, and deeds which are inconsistent with His guidance. In other words, we are sorry for our **sins**. The culmination of the Liturgy of the Word is the recitation of the **Creed** by the community: we restate our beliefs (i.e. refer to Appendix V. The Nicene Creed).

The Liturgy of the Eucharist is the second part of the Mass and focuses on the sacrifice Jesus made to redeem us from our sinful actions. This redemption, or saving action by Jesus, opened the door to Heaven for those of us who are willing to tell God we are sorry for our sins and who are willing to obey His commandments. During this part of the Mass the priest repeats the actions and words of Jesus during the Last Supper (Luke 22:14-23, Matthew 26:17-30, Mark 14:12-26). The priest in turn holds up the bread and then the cup of wine and says the following:

"... (Jesus) took bread and, giving thanks, broke it, and gave it to his disciples, saying:

**TAKE THIS, ALL OF YOU, AND EAT OF IT,
FOR THIS IS MY BODY,
WHICH WILL BE GIVEN UP FOR YOU.**

In a similar way, when supper was ended,
He took the chalice
and, once more giving thanks,
He gave it to his disciples, saying:

TAKE THIS, ALL OF YOU, AND DRINK
FROM IT,
FOR THIS IS THE CHALICE OF MY BLOOD,
THE BLOOD OF THE NEW AND ETERNAL
COVENANT,
WHICH WILL BE POURED OUT FOR YOU
AND FOR MANY
FOR THE FORGIVENESS OF SINS.
DO THIS IN MEMORY OF ME."

This action by the priest is done in accordance with the command of Jesus and consistent with the teaching of the Magisterium (the teaching authority of the Catholic Church). The result is an amazing miracle! The bread is changed into the actual body of Jesus and the wine is changed into the actual blood of Jesus!

Hard to believe? Yes, of course. Impossible to believe? Not if you have the information I have. Let me explain.

Countless saintly people have experienced what is referred to as **Eucharistic Miracles**. An example of one of these miracles is called the *"Miracle of Lanciano."* Around the year 750 AD, in the town of Lanciano, Italy, a priest was saying Mass. This priest had doubts about the true presence of Jesus in the consecrated bread and wine. So, during Mass, God gave that priest and the world a beautiful gift. The Bread became actual human flesh; the Blood became actual human blood. And what is even more interesting is that this flesh and blood remain alive and in that church today held in containers that make the miracle visible to pilgrims. The flesh and blood have been scientifically tested recently to verify their validity. This miracle at Lanciano and other Eucharistic miracles are explained in a video entitled **Miracles of the Eucharist** by Bob and Penny Lord.

My family has been blessed with our own Eucharist Miracle. During a pilgrimage to Medjugorje when she was a teenager, my daughter, Angela, was given a great gift from God. While attending Adoration during which the consecrated bread, the Eucharist, was exposed in a monstrance, Jesus spoke to her and said,

"It is I, Who am here. It is I, Who stands before you!
It is I, Who shall grant you your heart's desire."

Needless to say, this experience of seeking the Truth had a dramatic impact on her life. Praise God! Her encounter with our living Redeemer ultimately impacted her choice of spouse and her decision to bear spiritual fruit abundantly.

So, do I believe in the real presence of Jesus in the consecrated bread? Of course. Does it seem unreal? Yes. Is it logical from an ***unbeliever's*** point of view. No.

The image on the next page shows Saint Pope John Paul II holding the Eucharistic Jesus enclosed in a monstrance.

Eucharistic Jesus

Image Courtesy of http://www.turnbacktogod.com

It is impossible for me to attend daily Mass and leave without feeling a closeness to God. I leave Mass feeling connected to the Divine source of power. I leave feeling loved; I leave feeling safe and secure; I leave feeling centered; I leave feeling unified with Peace!

Sorry, I get a little carried away. It is difficult to talk about the Mass without going on endlessly. I should also tell you that, for many people, attending Mass may seem boring and even painful. I guess to them it might be like the first football game I observed. I was wondering why all those guys dressed in uniforms kept falling down. I did not really understand the "game." And so it is with Mass. The more you understand the game, the more interesting it is. I recently watched a movie about Saint Padre Pio, a priest who received the stigmata from God. *(Stigmata refers to the crucifixion wounds of Christ.)* Sometimes when he celebrated Mass it would last three hours! He understood the game; he understood Mass.

Fundamentally, Mass participation is nutrition for the soul of a Catholic. It is a vital component for a healthy spiritual life.

My next prayer of the day is the prayer of grace before meals. Ahhh! Breakfast. As I look with anticipation to the perfect meal delivered by my lovely wife I start to salivate. But before I attack the perfectly fried egg, the English muffin soaked in butter, the home-made bran muffin, and the hot apple juice, I say the prayer Catholics say before meals: "Bless us O Lord, and these Thy gifts, which we are about to receive from Thy bounty, through Christ our Lord, Amen."

After the meal, I say the Catholic prayer: "We give Thee thanks, O Lord, for these and all Thy benefits, which we have received from Thy bounty, through Christ, our Lord, Amen."

Grace is said before and after every meal throughout the day. We bless and we thank. Both are critical elements of our communication with God.

Occasionally I get a little carried away with this "thanks" when I have one of my favorite foods, such as Haagen-Dazs ice cream. In that case, the prayer might go something like this. "Thank You, God, for this amazing ice cream. Thank You for the cows that gave the cream. Thank You for the people who milked the cows. Thank You for the people who harvested the sugar cane. Thank You for the hard working people who harvested the vanilla beans in Madagascar. Thank You for the luscious vanilla bean taste! Thank You for the people who worked so hard to bring all the ingredients together and for the people who mixed everything into a divine concoction whose recipe was likely developed in Heaven itself. Thank You for my taste buds which are able to interact with the physical manifestation of the frozen elixir which provides a communication from You that is truly Divine! Wow!"

Now, keep in mind, one can thank God for numerous things throughout the day. I won't even start on Reese's Peanut Butter cups. If I did, I might run out of words.

The opportunity to thank God continues throughout the day. Frequently I remember to thank God for the people He has placed in my life: my parents, my wonderful and saintly wife, my amazing children, my incredible grandchildren, my friends, my church community, my relatives, and the religious who bring us the Sacraments. I also try to remember to thank God for placing in my life those people who cause me pain. Really? Yes, really. They are called "saint-makers." *(I admit that sometimes I forget this part of the prayer....)* Anyway, we should thank God in **all** things. ***There are no accidents!***

One technological advance which helps a lot when trying to pray constantly is the newer communication technology called Blue Tooth. One can actually walk through the mall these days and speak aloud to God in an ongoing conversation without people thinking you are crazy. If anyone notices you speaking to an unseen person, they just wonder where your microphone is hidden.

Okay, let's talk about petition prayer. This is when you ask God for something. <u>Does God answer your prayer?</u> Absolutely yes! <u>Every time.</u> He answers by saying, "Yes, no, or not now."

I chuckle when people thank God for answering their prayer of petition. That means He said, "Yes." What they don't understand is that you need to thank Him also when He says "No" and when He says "Not now." The fact is, since God is the perfect Father, He can only give you what is best for you at every moment of every day.

It is important to reflect on the truth of what I just stated. God

is <u>obliged</u> to give you what is best for you! Always! No Exceptions! He is the perfect parent! He is God! By His very nature, which is Love, He can only do what is in your best interests.

And remember, THERE ARE NO ACCIDENTS! That means, EVERYTHING that happens to you comes from God, either directly or indirectly.

You win a million dollars in the lottery. That is a gift from God. You get incurable cancer. That is a gift from God. You fall and break a leg. That is a gift from God. You are color blind from birth. That is a gift from God. You were abused as a child. That is a gift from God.

Okay, how can bad things be a gift from God?

Because God wants one thing to happen to you in this life. He wants you to choose Him and choose Heaven. Part of that decision process always involves pain. He uses pain and suffering to make you **more aware** of the choices you need to make and the suffering you can choose which ultimately leads to eternal happiness. For example, a married couple can choose to have a child which will cause them pain and suffering; but which also brings incredible joy in this life and in the next!

In my case, the way God most often speaks to me is called **Divine Providence**. Every situation and circumstance is orchestrated and monitored by God the Father. This happens constantly with me and with my family members. We often hear God's voice speaking to us through other people. **Awareness. Awareness. That is the key. Each person needs to be aware that God is speaking to us through people, events, nature, ideas, feelings, scripture, and so forth.** Let me give you two examples.

Near the end of my high school years, I was in the process of choosing a college. I had decided to attend the University of North Dakota. I was expecting to get a substantial scholarship from them. Meanwhile, my mom and our local priest were suggesting that I should consider attending Carroll College, a small, private Catholic College in Montana. As you might expect, the private college was quite a bit more expensive and I was responsible for paying my own way.

I am sure my mother and our priest said some serious prayers asking for God's intervention to get me to change my mind. Well, in my opinion He did get involved. It happened like this. The in-state college gave me a smaller scholarship than I was expecting. I was disappointed and offended by their offer. At the time it didn't occur to me that the lower offer was a sign from God. Anyway, I suddenly felt an overwhelming urge to change my mind and consider Carroll College. Within days I was signed up to attend Carroll and, at that moment, I experienced a deep sense of peace. *I now realize that it is the sense of peace one gets as confirmation from God that one has made the "right" decision — that is, the decision consistent with the will of God.*

And THANK GOD for that life-changing decision and His involvement in making it happen. It was that decision which allowed me to find the spouse that He wanted me to have — my beautiful and holy wife, Mary Hoff. Praise God! That decision allowed me to live an incredible life that I cannot find the words to express. It has been a miraculous experience. And it is still happening!

I'd like to share with you another example of when God spoke to me via Divine Providence.

My wife was convinced that one of my sons was doing drugs during his high school years. She was praying for him constantly. I tried to ignore the possibility even though there was plenty of evidence to confirm his drug usage.

It so happened that one day Mary and I were on the campus of the high school in the middle of the day to attend an event in which our daughter was involved. Suddenly we were confronted by a member of the school administration. Our son had been caught on campus with drugs in his possession. We were asked to remove him from the campus immediately.

Crisis time! My wife and I were in shock and felt devastated. Then as we were walking down the hallway towards the building exit, I glanced through an open door into an office. On the wall I saw one of the largest clocks I have ever seen in a small office. It was almost three feet high. The hands on the clock were showing EXACTLY 3:00 p.m., the hour of Divine Mercy, the hour of the death of our Lord Jesus Christ.

Instantly I **became aware** that **God was speaking to me** through this sign. In effect, He was saying, *"I've got this situation under control. Trust Me."*

I relaxed. I was in pain, but I was at peace.

The entire situation eventually evolved into a huge miracle. My son was kicked out of school for the few weeks remaining in the semester. Then, prior to the beginning of the second semester, the school administration invited my son, myself, and my wife to attend a meeting. In the meeting there were about ten people representing the school. My son was presented with an option: he could come back to school for the duration of the entire four month second semester... under the condition that he would be subject to random drug tests.

My son and I were taken to another room where we could discuss the proposal. When we were alone, I told him I would support his decision should he decide to stay, or support his decision should he decide to drop out. He struggled mightily with the alternatives. He was already addicted. He knew it would be nearly impossible for him to go four months without drugs. Also, he was not doing that well academically.

I did not push either alternative. Frankly, I was not sure what God wanted. So I left the decision entirely up to him.

There was a knock on the door. We were being asked to return to the meeting where my son was directed to indicate his decision.

He calmly and humbly addressed the school authorities. He said, "Okay. I will accept the option to return to school. I am willing to submit myself to the random drug testing."

Whew! As a loving father, I was relieved and terrified. The decision was wonderful, but I didn't think he was capable to living up to his commitment.

During the next three months, my son refrained from drugs completely. There was only one month to go. My wife kept praying intensely. His grades had improved dramatically. The miracle was happening....

Then we received word from the school principal. She wanted to see my son and his parents. We met with her. She was very emotional. She was fighting back tears. She told us that she was amazed that our son had kept his commitment regarding drugs and had done so much to improve his academics. She said, "Based on your record this past three months, you are no longer subject to the random drug tests the final four weeks of this semester."

It was celebration time! My son continued doing well to complete that year. Eventually he graduated from high school with decent grades, was accepted into college where he achieved excellent grades, was honored by being selected to become a resident assistant, graduated with a meaningful degree, and married a wonderful woman who loves him deeply.

Now with every miracle there are sometimes a couple of minor glitches. We didn't find out until later that, after the high school principal removed the threat of the random drug test, my son celebrated by smoking some pot that same night.... But, after all, is it not human nature in spiritual growth to take ten steps forward and then fall three steps back?

My son did learn from this entire experience of getting caught with drugs in school that he had a *choice.* As is usually true, the choice was between two painful options. Thank God he realized that he could *decide* to take a different path and not be a slave to drugs!

So this story is meant to give an example of how God can communicate to us via Divine Providence; in this case it was a clock that showed me the hour of Divine Mercy at the exact moment I needed it! By seeing the 3:00 p.m. time on the clock, I was instantly at peace about the situation and knew God had everything under control. I did not have to worry. But to receive God's message, I had to *be aware!* I had to be aware that He is *always communicating* to each of us in some way. Pay attention!

Now let me get back to my prayer life.

After my morning experience of prayer with God, the remaining communication with God during the day is ad hoc. It is usually not planned. Sometimes I travel to a local church that has perpetual

Eucharistic Adoration. There I visit with Jesus and do some spiritual reading. Also, my Guardian Angel will frequently make me aware that it is 3:00 p.m., which is the hour Jesus died. When that happens, I say, "For the sake of His sorrowful passion, have mercy on us and on the whole world." *(This is a portion of the Divine Mercy prayer that Jesus gave to Saint Sister Faustina.)* When I feel some stress, I use another prayer Jesus gave her: "Jesus, I trust in You."

At other times during the day I frequently thank God for His blessings.

At this stage of my life, since I am retired from "work" that generates a salary, I have extra time. This allows me to respond to requests from my wife to help her or help her help others. This type of prayer is called "service." My wife is very tuned into the needs of others, particularly our family and friends. Usually this means that I can be obedient to God by being obedient to her requests and suggestions. Despite some initial complaining on my part, in the end I get the sense of peace that I am doing the will of God. My initial complaining is merely the humanity in me that is not yet purified. God is still creating me, with my cooperation!

Finally, in the evening, I briefly reflect on the day and identify any thoughts, words, or deeds that require me to ask God for forgiveness. I also repeat the prayer I say in the morning: "Lord, please help me to do Your will tomorrow. And please give me the wisdom to know Your will. Amen."

In summary, my urgent advice on this topic is that you develop your own unique prayer life and pray "constantly" to stay in communication with our heavenly Father and follow faithfully the promptings of the Holy Spirit.

Obedience; not Success

I mentioned Saint Sister Faustina. Let me give you more background on this recently canonized saint.

Sister Faustina was a Catholic Nun from Poland. She was a mystic. She had visions of Jesus during her life. Her conversations with Him were captured in her diary. Sister Faustina died at the age of thirty-three in 1938.

Sister Faustina was canonized by the Catholic Church on April 30, 2000. She is venerated within the Church as the "Apostle of Divine Mercy".

Saint Sister Faustina's Diary is published and is entitled **Divine Mercy in My Soul**. It is a spiritual classic. I highly recommend you read it.

In her book, at numbered paragraph 28, Sister Faustina describes a situation and associated conversations she had with Jesus. Jesus tells her to ask her Superior for permission to perform a mortification (a suffering) by wearing a painful hair shirt. **Her superior refuses to allow this.** When Sister Faustina conveyed her response to Jesus, He said, "I was here during your conversation with the Superior and know everything. **I don't demand mortification from you, but <u>obedience</u>.** By obedience you give great glory to Me and gain more for yourself."

What does this mean? I believe that what Jesus is telling Sister Faustina, and indirectly all of His followers, is that **our goal is to be obedient to the promptings of the Holy Spirit. Jesus is telling us that the only <u>meaningful</u> achievement or success in His Kingdom is obedience to the requests of God. Our immediate reward is the peace of mind that comes with that accomplishment.**

A similar reference to this concept is found in the Bible, Matthew 6:3. Jesus says that when we help people, **our right hand should not know what our left hand is doing.** He is telling us that our goal is to be so docile to the Lord that we do His work in blissful unawareness. The challenge of assessing one's own actions in this regard is self evident. However, I will briefly mention here some situations that came to my awareness. I believe they relate to this topic.

After my conversion whereby I committed to obey God 100%, I was bursting with the Holy Spirit. I had no fear. I could discern clearly evil influences in the life of my family.

One of the first things I did was to move the TV set to the attic, and replace it with a small plastic statue of the Blessed Virgin Mary.

Then I told my family I was going to quit my high-paying IBM job and become an evangelist. I also prepared them for the possibility that this might mean that eventually we would have to sell our nice, big, beautiful house in Westchester County, New York, and move to the ghetto and live with the poor people.

Guess what? My family was not ready for that level of commitment. I was intending to be obedient, but the vote was 10 to 1 against my plans. My lovely, faithful wife, who had prayed for twenty-five years for my "conversion," was suddenly telling my kids that I was crazy.

And perhaps I was. At that instant, I was crazy enough to think that God was going to speak to *me* directly and *not* also speak to, and through, my loving family. *(A serious lesson in humility.)* I suddenly became *more aware* that, as part of my discernment of God's will, I needed to consider the family as *one organism.* The response to God had to be consistent with where we were as a *family unit* in our *journey of faith.* It was not my role as a father to journey independently. It would be irresponsible of me to ignore or coerce my wife and kids as the family unit journeyed forward.

Another action I took, which was uncharacteristic of me, was to give a friend and business associate a religious book that I had just read. It was about the Apparitions taking place in Medjugorje.

A few days later I was alone with my friend and he was very emotional. From his perspective, the book was a message from God and from the Blessed Virgin Mary. *(And he was right, of course.)* Today my friend is a Deacon in the Catholic Church. As for me, my right hand didn't know what my left hand was doing. I had no idea that God was going to work a miracle through a simple, oblivious act on my part.

God performed another miracle through an oblivious me. I found out about it after the fact. A single person who was very close to me was involved in a serious and sinful relationship with someone who was already married with kids. I was completely unaware of this situation. Circumstances developed whereby we were alone and we had a normal conversation. What I didn't realize is that the conversation was occurring at two levels. I was just chatting with no agenda in mind. The other person assumed that I knew about the spiritually deadly situation and was receiving advice which was coming out of my mouth. It could only have been the Holy Spirit. I have no idea what actual words were exchanged.

Anyway, it wasn't until a couple of months later that I was told that the deadly relationship *(which I knew nothing about)* was terminated "based on the advice I had given." Wow! Amazing!

It goes without saying that, had I known about the deadly situation and tried to direct the outcome, I would likely have failed miserably.

My advice: pray and ask God for the gift of obedience. And if you dare, you can also ask for the gift of humility. *(Warning: I prayed for humility once; and after 24 hours I told God to cancel the prayer....)*

Childhood Decisions

So if you committed to obey God's will, then you should continue reading. If you haven't made that primal decision, and said "yes" to God, then the rest of this advice becomes somewhat academic. It is like a map given to a sailor that has large holes in it. Without that first primal decision of "yes," you could run aground and die. I am not trying to scare you; I am just trying to communicate Reality.

You will make one huge decision when you are about 18 years old. The question will be, "Which college should I attend?" Following that you will make another huge decision, "Who should I marry?"

But before we get into these huge decisions, let us talk a little bit about the decisions you need to make earlier in life. Let us start with your childhood up to the age of 13.

You should operate on the assumption that until you are at least 13 years old, you can discern God's will by a listening to your parents. For all practical purposes, they will communicate to you God's will.

They will tell you that you should not lie, you should not steal, you should not take another person's toys, you should share your possessions, you should help around the house, you should be kind to your brothers and sisters, you should pray regularly, you should eat healthy foods, you should exercise to maintain a healthy body, you should study hard in school, and so forth.

Important decisions you make during your childhood are often related to your friends. Your parents will help you choose friends *who are healthy for you. They will try to have you spend time with friends who have the same <u>values</u> that they want you to have.*

Most likely many of you who are reading this book have already passed this childhood stage of your life. If your parents read this book first, they probably determined that you will benefit the most by being at least thirteen-years-old when you read it. However, if you are thirteen or older, you should reflect for a moment on your childhood and think about how you followed your parents' advice. Ask yourself the question, "Are my parents generally happy with my behavior? Or do I have some major issues that I know should be corrected?"

Now I understand that not all parents are perfect, so there may be some special circumstances in which you have an honest disagreement with them. If that happens, and if I am still alive, come and talk to me. Or talk to your grandma. That is why you have grandparents.

Just remember, I love you very much. Your grandma loves you very much. And your parents love you very much and want what is best for you. Our extra experience in life contributes to our perspective. We are all striving for Heaven, and we all want what is best for *you*. We want *you* to make your *primal decision* to consciously strive for Heaven by *committing 100%*. We want for you what God wants for you, which is to be with your family and friends in Heaven for eternity.

Teenage Decisions

So now let us talk about your teenage years. *You will be making many decisions during this period of your life. I would venture to say that it will be the most traumatic time of your life.*

From Rules to Relationships

This is the stage of your life when you naturally transition your focus from *__rules__ to __relationships__*. What does that mean?

Think about it. What are the *rules* your Catholic parents give you to survive these turbulent years.

Parents rules for teenagers:

- Do not smoke
- Do not drink
- Do not take illegal drugs
- Do not be deceitful
- Do not dress immodestly
- Do not engage in impure thoughts, words, or deeds
- Do not have sex before marriage

Does this sound a little like the Ten Commandments given to us in the Bible by the God of the Old Testament? Jesus refers to these rules and many other less meaningful rules as "the Law." The *focus* of the *Law*, that is, the *focus* of the *Rules*, is to tell you what *NOT* to do. The idea is to identify those actions which are unhealthy and to instruct you on what to avoid. Furthermore, if you do them, you are, by definition, sinning against God.

So, teenagers, what's the problem? Let us all just follow these rules. We should just follow the rules like the Israelites of the Old Testament followed the Ten Commandments.... Whoops!... I just remembered.... The Israelites spent most of their existence breaking the rules with great regularity. ...And, it turns out, it is the same for most humans alive today (*perhaps even your parents!*). **Everyone is breaking the rules all the time. So what's the answer?** The answer can be found in Saint Paul's letter to the Galatians, Chapters 3-5. His point is paraphrased as follows:

> **Jesus is the answer. He <u>became</u> the Old Law and died on the cross to put that Law to death and, by His resurrection, <u>fulfilled</u> the Old Law and created a world which operates under a New Law: the Law of Love. <u>The New Law of Love is all about relationships!</u>**

What I just stated is critically important. You may need to re-read the above statement a few hundred times over several years to really understand it and accept it. The statement gives the reality of spiritual growth whereby we **transition from <u>rules</u> to <u>relationships</u>**. As a teenager, you instinctively know this. You are torn between what appears to be two conflicting paths: obedience to your "godly" parents or obedience to your natural instincts to hang out with your (sinful) teenage peers. The focus on the new **Law of Love** (*which could also be called the* **Law of Freedom**) is that you no longer need to focus on the "thou shalt not" rules. You need to focus on the **relationship** you have with your parents, your peers, and yourself. You must also focus on your relationship with God your Father, Jesus your Brother, and Mary your spiritual mother. You will then become **<u>aware</u>** that **if you break the rules (the Law), you are hurting everyone who is connected to you in a relationship, including the relationship you have with <u>yourself</u>! Moreover, success is achieved NOT by your adherence to the rules, but rather by your <u>faith</u> that <u>you are a child of God</u>. <u>God is YOUR</u>**

<u>FATHER</u>. <u>*He loves you no less if your break the rules!*</u> This is why the Law of Love can also be called the Law of Freedom. No matter what you do, God is still your Father and He still loves you. That is a remarkable fact. ***That is a life-changing perspective.***

Now don't misunderstand. I am not suggesting that you go through life breaking the rules. What I am saying is that ***if*** you succumb to temptation and break the rules, ***then*** you should run to your Father, tell Him you're sorry, and let Him comfort you. You are His child that He created in His image. ***<u>Decide</u>*** to become the Prodigal Son and humbly return home (Luke 15:11-32). Your Father will be there, pacing the floor, waiting for you. As a Catholic, you have the Sacrament of Confession to effect this reconciliation.

As a parent, that is, as a human father who knows the pain caused by sin, I joined my virtuous wife in informing my teens about "the Law," that is, the Rules for teenagers. The problem is that the only way we could force our teens to obey the law was to lock them in their room for the seven years of their teenage life. Most of them objected to that option. The next best option was to make them aware that they could be "in" the world but not "of" the world. In other words, we allowed them to associate with their "sinful" friends, but prayed fervently that they would resist the temptation to join them in unhealthy behaviors. In fact, we hoped that ideally our teens would influence their friends to grow spiritually. This decision to let our teens engage fully in life was extremely difficult. It took a great deal of *faith*.

I will readily admit that some of my most painful moments as a father were the times when one of my "perfect" sixteen-year-old daughters brought a sub-human slug home and introduced him to me as her date for the evening. It was terrifying from several points of view. It took every ounce of control I had to force a smile and say, "Hi! Pleased to meet you," when in fact I was overwhelmed with the urge to scream in agony, dash up to my bedroom, and wrap my head in a pillow.

I have more faith now than I did during those years. In fact, let me share a true story about my faith journey.

Immediately after my decision twenty-five years ago to commit myself 100% to doing God's will, I was filled with the Holy Spirit and felt ready to go on national TV to proclaim the Gospel. I had no fear. I had complete faith... or so I thought.

Shortly after God zapped me, a huge windstorm hit our area in New York state and one of my huge, beautiful spruce trees was blown over. It was an ugly sight. It was going to cost a lot to remove it.

God's word, however, came to my mind. Jesus says in scripture, "If you have faith as small as a mustard seed, you can say to this tree, 'Be uprooted and planted in the sea,' and it will obey you" (Luke 17:6). He also says, "If you have faith as small as a mustard seed, you can say to this mountain, 'Move from here to there,' and it will move. Nothing will be impossible for you" (Matthew 17:20). That promise was exciting news for me.

So, at 5:30 a.m. the next morning, I stood in my back yard facing the fallen tree as the sun was beginning to peek over the horizon. I looked all around to verify that no neighbor was outside... I didn't want to disturb them.... Then I spoke aloud in a measured tone, "Tree, stand up."

Nothing happened. So I tried again, but this time I spoke louder and injected a tone of authority, "Tree, stand up now!"

I waited. Again, nothing happened. I glanced around quickly to verify that there were no witnesses to my unsuccessful attempt to invoke God's power.

Did Jesus tell the truth? I didn't doubt His words. But I was somewhat depressed to think that my fledgling faith was smaller than a mustard seed, which is .04 millimeters in diameter. To be honest, I am not sure I have enough faith even today to make a tree stand up in that circumstance.

However, I was greatly encouraged about twenty years after that apparent failure when one of my daughters gave me a card for Father's Day with a handwritten note inside which said, "Dad, thank you for the *gift of faith* you passed on to me. *You showed me how to move mountains in my life!*"

Anyway, back to the point about moving from *rules to relationships*. The new world revealed by Jesus through his life, death, and resurrection gives us a new focus. Our focus needs to be on our *relationship* with God, other people, and ourselves.

If we understand the essence of our relationships and the peace and joy that comes from healthy, pure, and <u>intimate relationships</u>, we will automatically start making healthier decisions and avoid sinful thoughts and actions. We will automatically start following the rules!

The specifics of balancing your life as you transition from **rules to relationships** are beyond the scope of this book. However, I will repeat again the urgent advice: improve your relationship with God through constant prayer, and you are guaranteed to continue your journey in the right direction, consistent with the will of your Father in Heaven!

I referred above to **intimate relationships**. In the next section I want to talk more about the ***intimacy instinct*** that God built into every one of us.

The Intimacy Instinct

God built into us a desire for intimacy. God built into us the ultimate desire: <u>spiritual communion</u>. <u>This ultimate desire, this desire for spiritual communion, is at the root of all desire to be intimate with another being.</u> It is the desire to become "one" with God. To experience this intimacy with God is to experience Heaven.

The goal of spiritual intimacy with God is to become "one" with God. Jesus refers to this concept several times in scripture. Consider the following texts:

- John 10:30. "*The Father and I are one.*"

- John 10:38: "*...the Father is in Me and I am in the Father.*"

- John 14:15-20. "If you love Me, you will keep My commandments. And I will ask the Father, and He will give you another Advocate to be with you always, the Spirit of truth, which the world cannot accept, because it neither sees nor knows it. But you know it, because it remains with you, and will be in you. I will not leave you orphans; I will come to you. In a little while the world will no longer see Me, but you will see Me, because I live and you will live. ***On that day you will realize that <u>I am in my Father</u> and <u>you are in Me</u> and <u>I in you</u>***."

Starting with the Eucharist instituted at the Last Supper, Jesus said, ***"This is My Body; this is My Blood. Do this in memory of Me"*** (see Luke 22:19-20). He also says at another time, ***"Unless you eat the flesh of the Son of Man and drink His blood, you do not have life within you"*** (John 6:53). Whoa! What was that? Did He really say that? Did He really mean that?

Yes He did. He said it; He meant it. To deny that is to deny Reality. So how does this relate to spiritual communion, to intimacy?

Saint Paul, who was one of the most knowledgeable Catholics in the world at the time of Jesus, says that ***the Church is the "Bride of Christ"*** (2 Cor. 11:2). Well, guess what! If the Church is the Bride, and Christ is the Groom, what happens after the Wedding Ceremony? They become "one." They unite spiritually, intellectually, emotionally, and physically. The union occurs when we give ourselves to one another; it occurs when we swallow the consecrated bread, the Body of Christ, and drink the consecrated wine, the Blood of Christ.

Whew! Deep stuff. You may not have realized that God is extremely interested in achieving communion with his human creatures. For us to deny this instinct is the basic cause of harmful addictions. What? Addictions are related to lack of communion with God?

Think about it for a second. Think!

One of our most basic human desires is intimacy with God. Our inability to achieve fully that intimacy in this earthly life results in us looking for created alternatives. These alternatives are such things as mind-altering drugs, alcohol, caffeine, sex, power, food, and this list is virtually endless.

With addictions, the "substitute god" appears "good." We get pleasure initially. Then we need increasing amounts of this created good, this idol, to be satisfied. We become addicts. We become addicted to our false god. We worship this "god." This addiction in fact leads us further away from the real God, our Creator. We wallow in our addictions and are tempted beyond our ability to resist. We inexorably move down the path towards a living hell. This earthly hell is merely a shadow of the real Hell, which is eternal life without God, our Creator.

So what do I, an addicted person unable to get out of this death spiral, do next? I can't help myself. I want to head toward God, but the temptation is overwhelming. I need to sooth my pain of not having intimacy with God by indulging myself and engaging with my fake god, my idol, the object of my addition.

Well, there is only one way out. And it turns out it is quite simple. Humility. That is it. Humility. The antidote to the primal sin of pride. The primal sin of pride is when we humans want to "be like God." It is true of all of us (even me — ha!... And I say that in all humility...).

So the way out of an addiction is to accept the fact that "I" cannot win when fighting the addiction. The only way to fight an addiction is to recognize that there is a "higher power" *(which Catholics call God!)* who is capable of freeing me. "The Truth will set you free!" And the truth is that God is my Father, and God will reconcile everything. In fact, He has already done that by sending His Son, Jesus, to die for me on the cross and redeem me from evil.

So if He has already redeemed me, what is the problem?

Well, the problem is this. God has given us a life-giving gift. He has given us eternal life. But our ***choice*** is to ***accept*** that gift or ***reject*** that gift. The choice is whether we want to spend eternity in Heaven with Him, the good angels, and our "holy" brothers and sisters? Or whether we want to spend eternity suffering in Hell?

Why would anyone choose Hell?

Well, based on the way many people are living their lives today, one might observe that they have decided, perhaps subconsciously, to choose Hell. If I fail to acknowledge that "there is a God, and I am not Him," then I do not have the humility I need to join my family in Heaven. And if I decide that I am a god, then I make up my own rules. I can cheat, steal, bully, fornicate, practice adultery, lie, swear, gossip, and so forth. I can do all those things because I have created my own heaven... which God calls "Hell".

So, as Jesus says, *"Repent! The Kingdom of Heaven is at Hand"* (Matthew 4:17). In other words, be humble and change the direction of where you are headed. He is saying, *"Follow My advice and head towards intimacy with Me and my Father... and that is where you are ultimately fulfilled."* In Heaven, you will no longer be tempted by your addictions. Your tempter will be seen by you no more. You will experience "ecstasy"... the real one, not the illegal drug. You will be transported into spiritual intimacy with your Creator and with His holy creatures, your holy brothers and sisters. You will be in Heaven!

Amen!

Sexual "Freedom"

If you are a teenager and read the table of contents, you may have skipped directly to this section. Why? Because your hormones are going crazy. You want intimacy and your friends and the world around you are telling you that "sex" is the way to find intimacy. You are looking for that glow, that excitement, of a deeply personal interaction with another human. Many of you are looking for "freedom" from the rigid rules of your parents and your church.

I look at Haagen-Dazs ice cream in a similar way. I *lust* after it. When it is in front of me, I will always succumb to the temptation to consume it. I never eat less than one pint at a time. At other times I consume a quart. *(Although the manufacturer has started to cheat on the portions. A pint is now 14 ounces rather than 16, and a quart is now 28 ounces rather than 32.)*

So what's the problem? I have the freedom to eat as much Haagen-Dazs as I want. I can afford it. No one is forcing me to not eat it. God has not forbidden it, although I think somewhere He did mention something about gluttony being a problem.

*The reason I don't eat two quarts of Haagen-Dazs every day is that I can see **the bigger picture.*** I can see a vision of myself severely overweight suffering discomfort. I see a vision of myself whereby I can't see my shoes to tie them. *And then there is the reality of my gluttony* *that is <u>unseen</u>, and even more serious.* It's the long term consequences. My brother, John, a medical doctor, says that overeating can eventually result in diabetes and heart disease. He says that one of the major problems with diabetes is that cholesterol will build up in my arteries. The first 50% narrowing of the vessel is very gradual and may take 10 years. The last 50% can occur in an instant when the vessel clots off. The result can be a heart attack, stroke, blindness, or kidney failure. In other words, I can die! Or what may even be worse, I may live the remainder of my life in terrible misery!

Doctor John describes the big picture like this. Regularly overeating Haagen-Dazs is like jumping out of a 10 story building and, after falling 5 floors, exclaim, "I am doing great so far!"

So my vision of the big picture enlightens me. I understand that what seemed like a great idea of exercising my freedom will turn into a long nightmare of pain and suffering. *I understand that what <u>appeared</u> to be the road to "<u>freedom</u>" was actually the road to "<u>slavery</u>." That vision of the <u>big picture</u> is what gives me the <u>discipline</u> to control my circumstances and never allow the object of my desire to be readily available.* I cannot keep ice cream in my freezer!

So, you might ask, "How does Grandpa's lust for ice cream relate to my sex life? Could it be that there are some similarities? If so, what is the big picture regarding sex?"

The big picture is this. Believe it or not, according to the Bible, God created man "in His image." He created them male and female. The male and female are to become "one flesh" (see Genesis 2:24). Furthermore, this comm-<u>union</u> of the male and female is the visible sign of the invisible Reality of the intimate relationship between the three Persons of God. The relationship within the three Persons of God is an eternal Communion of Persons. Catholics believe that the love between the Father and the Son is so powerful and fruitful that the third Person, the Holy Spirit, proceeds from their union. The divine Persons mutually "give" themselves unconditionally in love and service. Furthermore, we believe that it is *God's plan that we humans are destined to share in that eternal exchange of love.* We believe that God has designed the *human <u>body</u>* in such a way as to reveal the innermost secret of our existence! *We believe that the <u>union of the sexes</u> reveals the "great mystery" of God and leads us into the heart of God's plan for the cosmos!*

Are you kidding me? Human sexuality reveals the innermost workings of God? Who came up with that idea?

Actually, it was a Pope who came up with that idea. Saint Pope John Paul II was inspired to develop the teachings called *"Theology of the Body."* The word "theology" means "the study of God." Thus the title of the teaching means that by studying the human body and sexual union, we will observe how God is revealing Himself and His plan for humans. The Pope's concept is so profound, however, that if one were to compare the philosophical notion of the Theology of the Body to the scientific notion of Einstein's Relativity Theory, they are both beyond the comprehension of most people. That is why we are blessed to have an author named Christopher West who has made it his life-long work to take the profound insight of the Pope and explain it more simply to those of us who are less than brilliant. While several books and other resources on this topic are available, I suggest a good starting point is *"Theology of the Body for beginners"* by Christopher West. Several points in my discussion here were taken from that work.

One key concept described by Mr. West is the "language of love." Christ's love has four qualities:

1. Christ gives his body *freely* (John 10:18)
2. Christ gives his body *totally*—unconditionally (John 13:1)
3. Christ gives his body *faithfully* (Matthew 28:20), and
4. Christ gives his body *fruitfully* (John 10:10)

If men and women understand and accept this language of love, their union will express the same *free, total, faithful, and fruitful* love that Christ's body expresses. They will be acting in accordance with God's "big picture."

My urgent advice is this. Understand that the world and some of your peers will try to convince you to binge on unhealthy spiritual food now and ignore the big picture. The big picture is that God has prepared a heavenly banquet for you that will ***fulfill completely*** all your yearnings for a deep, intimate, satisfying relationship which will vastly ***surpass*** your wildest expectations. But you can only reach that spiritual banquet if you aren't distracted by eating scraps from the shiny attractive dumpster with a blinking neon sign that is blocking your path. To overcome the temptation to eat out of the dumpster you need to:

- understand more about the spiritual banquet (the big picture),
- admit that you are eating unhealthy scraps, and
- ask God to give you the strength and ***discipline*** to overcome the distracting temptation.

If you continue to eat from the dumpster, and do not admit to the problem that confronts you, it is the same as jumping off a ten story spiritual building and exclaiming aloud as you fall past the fifth floor, "Everything is going great so far!"

Which College?

Okay, let's take a break from the deep stuff for a minute. Let's get very practical. Let's talk about your college decision.

Assuming that you survived your high school years and are not too messed up, one of the big final decisions you make as you near the end of high school is to choose a college.

Your choice of college will probably determine where you are going to live the rest of your life, who you are going to marry, and what your basic philosophy of life will be. Wow! That is really scary.

In making this decision, your parents will want to be heavily involved. This can be good and bad. It is a great idea to take advantage of their wisdom. On the other hand, whichever decision you make, ***you*** need to feel comfortable that it is ***your*** decision. If you do not take ownership of this decision, you are likely going to fail out of college, or be miserable.

One of the first and most practical considerations is cost. It is pretty unlikely that any of you will be able to afford the elite schools on the East Coast such as Harvard, Yale, Princeton, and so forth. California even has a couple of elite schools such as Berkeley and Stanford. While these are generally academically strong schools, you need very wealthy parents to be able to afford them.

Keeping in the financial realm, the next aspect of the decision is private college or public college. Generally speaking a public in-state college is a lot less expensive than a private college. If you attend a public college within the same state where you reside, the taxpayers in effect pay a portion of your tuition. This is one of the reasons why most of your parents attended public colleges in the State of New York where we were residents at the time.

Another key aspect of choosing a college is your decision about the type of education you want. For example, if your goal is to be an engineer, then you might find that attending a Catholic college focused on liberal arts inconsistent with that goal. It is not to say that you couldn't go to that college and eventually become an engineer; but it just makes the road harder and longer from a purely academic standpoint.

On the other hand, if you want to be a teacher or a priest or a nun, then a Catholic liberal arts college is a wonderful choice, assuming you can afford it.

And then there is the question of what God wants! I can only speak from personal experience. As I described earlier, my original intent was to attend a public state school in North Dakota and major in chemical engineering. Oh my goodness! If I had pursued that direction, my life would have been completely different. And I don't mean in the good sense.

But God had other plans. Since I didn't get the size of scholarship I was expecting, I rebelled against that state school and became open to the idea that my mother and my pastor were quietly recommending. They said almost nothing, but I sensed that they wanted me to attend Carroll College, a small, private Catholic college about 500 miles from my home. What was amazing is that once I made the decision to attend Carroll college, I was filled with an overwhelming sense of peace. That is God's way of confirming that I made a great decision. He gave me a sense of peace. Thank You, God!

By attending that small private Catholic college, which did cost more money, several things happened. The first thing I came to realize is that it is hard to be a chemical engineer if you are colorblind. I had an impossible time trying to do the lab exercises in chemistry when I was supposed to determine the color of various reactions when I mixed two different things together. I also had trouble in the first test when they said "What are you going to do if you are stuck on a deserted island with a bar of soap and some other items?" The only thing I knew about soap was that I could wash my armpits with it. I don't think that was the right answer.

So it turns out that I was taking a course in mathematics and was loving it. So I just majored in mathematics. This led me into computers and eventually into a thirty-six year job with the IBM Corporation, one of the largest and most successful businesses of its time.

Financially God took care of things also. One of my uncles died and shortly thereafter my Aunt Esther wanted to meet with me. She proceeded to loan me enough money to supplement what I had (which was nothing) so that I could continue my education at this private Catholic college. Thank you, Aunt Esther!

But the greatest gift that God gave me was infinitely more than the education which led to an excellent job. He gave me my partner for life: my lovely and holy wife, Mary Hoff. Wow! I can honestly tell you that if God had not placed her in my life I would likely have ended up similar to my father. I probably would have lived a miserable life and died at the age of fifty from alcoholism or some other serious addiction. Thank You, God!

The gift of my wife was one of those gifts that just keeps on giving. As we got married, we became one. The fruit of this oneness, given to us by God, was Christie, Angela, Nichole, Heidi, Robert, Ryan, Marianne, Russell, and Heather. And that was just phase one! Then came twenty-nine more gifts called grandchildren. And there may be more....

To recap, I am not suggesting everyone should attend a small, private Catholic college. I am just saying that it worked for me. I would suggest, however, that one of the decisions that helped many of my children to have a healthy outlook on their faith was to get involved with the Newman Club at the public university. This was basically the Catholic club at the University. In the case of the University of Binghamton in New York, this was the small but active group of Catholics on a large secular campus.

The experience of my son, Rob, may be of interest to you. He attended Franciscan University in Steubenville, Ohio. While there, Rob was influenced by his roommate, Luke, to make a pact to abstain from drinking alcohol until they reached age twenty-one. However, after his first year at Steubenville, Rob changed his course of study and needed to switch to a public college in Massachusetts: Worcester State College.

Shortly after Rob arrived at Worcester, his new college, he attended an off-campus party in order to meet new people. Despite the "party atmosphere," Rob was committed to maintain his "no drinking" pact.

When Rob arrived at the party, he noticed a young female student dressed in gothic garb sitting on the couch. Her face was white with makeup, her fingernails had black polish, she was wearing black lipstick, and her hair was combed straight up and was being held there with a heavy dose of hairspray. The girl was dangling a Rosary around her outstretched hands and was examining it. She seemed to be mesmerized by the shiny beads.

Rob introduced himself and asked to sit next to her on the couch. She said, "Okay."

Rob then asked, "Why are you holding the Rosary?"

She replied, "It belonged to my grandmother. I think it is beautiful."

Rob asked, "Do you want to learn how to pray the Rosary?"

The young woman replied politely, "Sure."

Rob decided to first teach her the Hail Mary prayer, since once you learn that prayer, you are 90% of the way towards learning the Rosary.

As Rob was teaching the girl to pray the Hail Mary, other students formed a circle on the floor near the couch, adjacent to their feet. The circle of students started passing around a joint. As the girl was praying aloud her second Hail Mary, she said, "Hail Mary, full of grace, ..." and paused to take a big hit of the joint that was being passed around.

Rob quickly realized he wasn't at Franciscan University any more. He looked up to the Heavens and declared to God, "You have a big job ahead of You, Big Guy!"

Later that evening, Rob reflected on how much he missed the positive peer influence that existed on the campus of the orthodox Catholic college of Franciscan University. Then God revealed to him that you need to meet people and build rapport if you want to bring to them the love of Christ. As a result of this insight, every meal of the day Rob made a determined effort to sit with a new group of students until he had met every student on campus.

It is not surprising that Rob was soon given a nickname. The students referred to him as "Reverend Rob."

To gain insight of how God worked in Rob's life, I strongly recommend you listen to his testimony which can be found on my website at **www.calltobefree.com**.

In the final analysis, you need to pray diligently about your college decision. Listen to God and make a decision you feel is consistent with God's will. When you are *at peace* with the decision, then you will know you're making the right decision.

College Age Decisions

Okay. So now you are in college. What are the key decisions that you face during this exciting time of your life? And remember, these decisions should be made consistent with your primal decision: to obey God 100% the rest of your life!

College Age Decisions - What is the objective of college?

Your primary objective in attending college is to get a degree so that you can make an income to support your desired lifestyle as an adult upon graduation.

Your secondary goal is to interact with members of the opposite gender to discover the attributes you find important in identifying your future spouse.

The following is what college is **NOT**:

- A place to party constantly
- A place to squander your money or your parents' money
- A place to squander your time
- A place to experiment with unhealthy behaviors
- A place to overeat fattening foods
- A place to reject all your parents' advice
- A place to be brainwashed by atheistic or amoral professors.

College Age Decisions - Reprogramming the Home button

The biggest shock when you leave home to attend college is the sudden absence of the "Home" button. Let me explain.

You have lived at home for your entire life. Because of that, you may take certain things for granted, such as:

- Food
- Shelter
- Clothing
- Car
- Spending money
- Family love
- Structured daily routine.

Now some of these things may continue in college. But the biggest change will likely be the structured daily routine. Suddenly your parents are not there to make you get up in the morning and convince you to attend classes. They are not there to make sure you hang out with healthy friends and get home at decent hour, arriving sober. They are not there to make sure you eat healthy meals. And the list goes on.

Your first reaction: "Great! Free at last! Free at last! Thank God, I am free at last!"

Your reaction at the end of the first semester: "Darn! My grades are horrible, I have gained fifteen pounds, I am a pothead, I am depressed, and if this continues I will flunk out of college and have to work for minimum wage for the next fifty years until I die."

So what is the solution?

Guess what? *You have to become your own parent!* You have to become the type of person you rejected and rebelled against in so many ways. You have to become a parent to yourself and learn to *discipline yourself!*

Sorry. I am not kidding. The only way you will survive and eventually become the person that you are meant to be is to become a morphed, upgraded version of your parents.

Oh, my goodness. Can this possibly be true?

Let me mention briefly my experience as the parent of a child who just started college. *(Now to put this in context, the way people communicated in those ancient times was by letters written on paper with ink and then mailed using the United States Postal System.)* About six weeks into the first semester, the letter would arrive from the college newbie. The message went like this: "Gee, Mom and Dad. I really miss home. I really appreciate everything you have done for me. I can't believe how many kids here at school have messed up parents. I am very grateful for what you taught me growing up. Love, your son/daughter. PS. I am running out of money. Everything cost so much."

Yes, you will likely write such a message. Be humble. It is okay to let your parents know that they are good people. You will not regret making the decision to send this message.

College Age Decisions - Party and Prayer Strategy

Other than the academics, there are two ongoing decisions that need to be addressed: your party strategy and your prayer strategy.

You will have endless opportunities to party at college. As a general strategy you may want to attend some parties so that you have some social life. Be aware that there are different kinds of parties. They vary by the degree to which mind-altering drugs are available and the type of activities that are involved. My advice is as follows. When you attend a party, refrain from consuming anything stronger than a soft drink, dress modestly, be among the first to leave, and travel in groups if you are a female.

You will observe in college that the morals you were taught at home are not accepted by most of your peers. The temptation: "Why not do it? Everyone else is doing it?"

The danger here is the assumption that God grades on the curve. The unstated assumption is that, if I am not as immoral as some of the others, I will make the cut and pass the test for Heaven.

Bad thinking! This is a losing strategy designed for you by your very intelligent enemy, Satan. Reject it immediately. You do not want to forfeit your eternal happiness by accepting an arrogant assumption.

Now what about your prayer strategy?

You have been raised Catholic by your parents. You were taught that the right thing to do is to attend Mass every Sunday in order to thank God for everything and to re-commit yourself to obeying His advice. A huge temptation in college is to decide to miss Mass. Danger, danger, danger. One miss becomes two. Three misses and now a habit is formed. Eventually you get out of range of God's cell-phone signals directed to you. It goes downhill (to Hell) from there.

Discipline is needed! Attend Mass. Make friends with other kids who are attending; they likely have similar values to yourself. Join a campus Catholic group. Join a Catholic group that serves others in some capacity if possible. Pray often.

College Age Decisions - Finding a Spouse

College is a great time to look for a future husband or wife. It is a fairly straightforward process.

Where do you start? Simple. Identify the other students who attend Mass on Sunday. Identify those who attend daily Mass. Interact with these future Saints and find the one that God has chosen for you from the beginning of time.

Obviously not everyone is called to marriage. You could be called to religious life or the single life. Stay in constant contact with God and He will lead you to your true vocation.

College Age Decisions - Finding a Job

As you engage in your academics at college, remember your goal. First of all, it goes without saying that you want to obey God's will. Beyond that you need to make the practical decision about your major course of study. For example, do I want to major in education, history, sociology, engineering, music, computers, biology, business, accounting, medicine, communications, philosophy, and so forth. Look at three factors here:

1. What do I enjoy doing?
2. What kind of jobs are available in this discipline?
3. Will the pay scale for this job support my desired lifestyle?

In addition, try to speak with someone who is doing this kind of work. Better yet, spend some time doing an internship in your field of interest.

By the time you near college graduation, you want to have had several interviews with companies that come to the college looking for recruits. This is fun if you have made a good decision regarding your major. If you majored in something like history or biology, you may have to go on to graduate school to convert your education into some specific profession, such as teaching or nursing.

Adult Decisions

Okay. You have graduated from college, or are about to graduate. What next? You are entering the marathon of life. How do you pace yourself so that you successfully finish the race and receive your crown from God?

Adult Decisions - Spouse Selection

You have entered the phase of your life where you will be making a decision about your spouse. Ask yourself the following questions. "Should I marry God and become a religious or single person? Or should I look for a member of the opposite gender and get married?" This is probably the second most important decision of your life (the first was the primal decision to obey God).

Pray a lot about this. Be aware of where God is leading you. Don't rush a decision. Be open to advice from friends and family.

Choose someone with similar values. If possible, choose someone with the same religion because then you will have the same framework for making decisions. It will be much easier to live out your faith and practice your beliefs. Select someone you enjoy just being around. Find a person who will be your **best friend** and who you enjoy being with 24 hours a day and 7 days a week. Select someone with whom you trust with your life. **Select the person who God has chosen for you.** Be mindful that, for all practical purposes, the person you see now is the person you will have for the rest of your life. Do NOT expect your future spouse to somehow magically change after you are married. Try to find someone who is already a practicing saint!

You will know you have made the right decision when you feel at **peace** with it.

Adult Decisions - Marriage

You selected your future spouse, and you are getting married. Remember, you are committing to remain married to this person "until death do you part!" If you are a faithful Catholic, divorce is not an option. And I can assure you, you will have highs and lows in your marital relationship, and the Enemy will be persistent in suggesting that divorce is a wonderful solution during the lows. The Enemy succeeds in selling this temptation about 50% of the time in our culture. Sad.

Here is the deal. The objective of marriage is *not* to live a pain-free pleasure-filled life. Rather, marriage is an institution that will allow you to grow in virtue and allow you to experience eternal bliss in the next life. Your focus is to help your spouse and kids get to Heaven. This will be a lot of work and you will need a lot of faith to persevere. You will make hundreds of choices to serve your family rather than serve your own selfish desires. Every day you will make many decisions to serve. This is called love! Marriage is designed to help you grow in your ability to love others by causing pain to yourself. Yes, seriously. Let me emphasize that assertion.

Marriage is designed to help you grow in your ability to love others by sacrificing yourself for them.

Finally, when you do have lows in your marriage, you will need a lot of prayer. You might even need some marriage counseling. But you absolutely need a faith-filled Catholic marriage counselor if you do this. Otherwise, the counselor will consider divorce as an option and lead you astray.

Lest these previous insights sound too negative, I need to confirm that marriage can be an incredible fulfilling adventure and tons of fun. As a parent and grandparent, you receive immense rewards as you watch your human creations, your kids and grandkids, engage in Life and Love. They play, they work, they pray, they sing, they dance, they hug, they laugh, they cry, they serve, they LIVE and they LOVE. Wow! And they are all a result of your cooperation with the Giver of Life and Love....

So just stay the course; attempt to do God's will always; appreciate your family relationships; laugh at everything; love your spouse deeply; and allow the Light to shine through you.

Adult Decisions - Family Planning

Once you are married, you and your spouse will implement your family planning decision. How many kids does God want us to have?

Certainly you discussed this prior to marriage. In case you are unaware, the Catholic Church will not allow you to receive the Sacrament of Matrimony unless you are open to having children. The Church, in her wisdom, teaches that marriage and procreation are inseparable.

The Church does not tell you how many children you should have. What she does tell you is that any decision to restrict the number you have should not be based on selfish reasons. In other words, you should not say, "I am going to have one less child so that I can get a huge TV set... new car... a bigger house... a vacation in Europe... and so forth."

What the Church does recommend is that in the circumstances whereby a faithful married Catholic couple wants to delay pregnancy temporarily due to physical or mental health issues, they should consider the **Natural Family Planning** technique. This Natural Family Planning technique has tremendous advantages in elevating the marital act to include the spiritual, intellectual, and emotional dimensions in addition to the physical dimension.

Young couples who are looking for good advice about how to achieve marital happiness should consider the adult book **Good News About Sex & Marriage** by Christopher West. *(I mentioned this author in the teenage chapter.)* **He provides the "big picture" and explains** the *"why" behind the "what"* of the spiritual roadmap to the heavenly banquet. He simplifies the Theology of the Body teachings by Saint Pope John Paul II to help us understand **God's design** for men and women desiring **intimate unity** with one another, with family, and with the Holy Trinity for eternity.

Adult Decisions - Teamwork and Sacrifice

You may have heard the expression, "Marriage is a 50-50 proposition." What people are saying when they repeat this expression is that each partner needs to complete the team by sharing 50% of the work. WRONG! **Marriage is a 100-100 proposition!** If you are living in this marital relationship and are calculating the 50% of work and responsibility that is yours, your marriage will fail miserably. Why? Because the only way to succeed and become "one" is for each partner to be willing to do 100% of everything. You both work until the work is done. Neither of you rests until the other can rest. **You are two bodies with one mind and heart**.

As a corollary to this, when you choose to buy things or engage in some entertainment, every decision must be made with your partner in mind. For example, I should take my wife out to Japanese food for dinner if she desires, even though the only thing I find tolerable on the menu is white rice. Similarly, my wife may decide to attend a movie with me that consists of several car chases, even though she would prefer a sappy girl movie where the girl and the guy spend two long movie hours in some form of emotional unfulfilling interaction.

Once kids arrive on the scene, then each couple has to agree 100% on the "rules" you employ for teaching the necessary disciplines. Do I physically spank the kids if they mess up, or do I send them to their room. *(Oh, yeah. I guess they frown on spankings now. I just threw that in to see if you were awake!)*

One of the basics here. Every child needs to grow in discipline. It takes a lot of love and a lot of work, but it MUST be done. Neither of you can be the "good guy" at the expense of the other. One basic instinct the child has from birth is "divide and conquer." Don't fall into that trap.

Adult Decisions - Family Life

As a family you need "together" time. The most practical way to meet this requirement is to eat dinner together every evening if possible. It should be a sit-down meal with no distractions, such as phone calls or text messaging. There should be one conversation, with everyone invited to participate. There should be eye-to-eye contact. There should be discussions about what is happening in the life of every person at the table. There should be the blessing of food said before the meal and a thanksgiving prayer said after the meal. Manners should be taught and used during the meal. After the meal, everyone should assist in the cleanup. Never, ever should a family meal be consumed in front of a TV.

Family events should be identified and scheduled. This might include trips to the zoo, campouts, hikes, vacations, concerts, and so forth. Dad, vegetating in front of TV all weekend is NOT an option. Sorry.

Parents, you need time alone. Every moment of your lives can be focused on your children. That is normal. But you need time alone with one another to rekindle your marital relationship. Dad, the wife NEEDS to get out and get away from the kids. She needs attention! She needs an adult conversation. She needs to feel loved and appreciated. Mom, the husband just wants to veg out after a stressful week at work. Be sensitive about giving him a long list of to-do's and a long list of complaints and problems. He needs to feel loved unconditionally and to feel respected and appreciated.

Adult Decisions - Communication

One of the most critical processes undertaken by a couple in marriage is communication. Over time it is natural that a major undiagnosed problem will develop. For that reason I strongly recommend that you buy, read, and study the book *Men are from Mars, Women are from Venus* by John Gray, Ph.D. The author has researched extensively how men and women differ in how they communicate. He also explains how they think, feel, perceive, react, respond, love, need, and appreciate differently.

This understanding of these differences helps resolve much of the frustration in dealing with, and trying to understand, the opposite sex. Misunderstandings can then be quickly dissipated or avoided. Incorrect expectations are easily corrected. When you remember that your partner is as different from you as someone from another planet, you can relax and cooperate with the differences instead of resisting or trying to change them.

The advice I found profoundly helpful as a man is to understand that when a woman complains it is best to listen intently and show empathy. It is important to resist the instinctive urge to solve the problem.

Some important advice that applies to a woman is the way in which a man deals with stress. He withdraws into his cave. A woman should never go into a man's cave or she will be burned by the dragon!

I will let the author of the book explain everything in a more coherent and detailed way. But I am convinced that every married couple could benefit greatly by reading this book and following the practical advice.

Adult Decisions - Forgiveness

Jesus says in the Bible during His Sermon on the Mount discourse, "Forgive your enemies." How true! He repeats that concept when He gives us the Lord's Prayer (the Our Father).

So who is your enemy? The radical terrorists in the Middle East who want to cut off your Christian head? No. Your enemy is your spouse!... What? Are you kidding?

Your enemy is your spouse. Why? Because your spouse can hurt you the most. You want to meet the needs of your spouse and you want to satisfy his or her needs. And if your spouse responds in such a way as to hurt your feelings, you will feel terrible. And beyond that, you may feel resentful if your spouse is critical and you think their judgment against you is not justified.

Big problem. You can react in different ways, but often your hurt and resentment buries itself in your psyche and hides itself in your subconscious. Then the Enemy quietly reminds you subconsciously of the injustice and you begin to treat your loving partner in an unloving way. The war escalates.

Forgiveness is the answer. I suggest that, as a matter of habit, you forgive your spouse several times a day.

You might even be married to a Saint, but, nevertheless, you must forgive your spouse frequently (Jesus says seventy-seven times). The fact is many times the problem is not the spouse, but rather the problem is yourself. It turns out that the forgiveness process works whether the problem is the other person or the problem is with you. Amazing! I think I learned this after fifty years of marriage. Hopefully it takes you less time to understand this wonderful advice from Jesus.

Adult Decisions - Peace and Joy

As Jesus said to the mystic I referenced in the Primal Decision section of this book, "If you commit to obey Me, you will have peace and joy."

I can vouch for that! I feel like I can shout that truth from the rooftops! Just obey the commandments of God that He gave us through the Bible and through our assigned leaders, the Pope and the Bishops, and you will have peace and joy.

The Spiritual War

Like it or not, God placed each of us on the battlefield in the midst of a Universe-wide war. Here is what we know as a result of the Bible and the teaching authority of the Catholic Church.

When God created the Universe, He created beings called Angels. Angels are spiritual beings who do not have bodies like humans. But they do have intelligence and free will. Since they are not bound by the laws of matter, they can virtually "fly around." Furthermore, since they do not have a "fallen nature" as does man, they can see and understand Reality more clearly than humans. They are fully aware of the existence of God and the Spiritual and Physical laws that exist in His Kingdom, both on earth and in Heaven.

According to the tradition of the Church, at the beginning of creation an Angel named Lucifer rebelled against God and said, "I will not serve." One third of the Angels joined him in that rebellion. We call them the "bad Angels" or "demons." We often refer collectively to the demons as Satan or the Devil. At other times we may use the term Satan or Devil to refer to Lucifer himself.

There are three Angels we know by name from the Bible who are good Angels: Gabriel, Michael, and Raphael. In fact, they are called Archangels to signify that they have a more critical role than that of a regular Angel. Gabriel was the Archangel who announced to Mary that she was going to be the Mother of God (the Mother of Jesus). The Archangel Michael is considered to be the Angelic leader in the Battle against Lucifer and his bad angels. The Archangel Raphael is mentioned in the Book of Tobit and is associated with healing. Since all the good Angels are in Heaven, they are also given the title of "Saint."

On a personal note, I pray to Saint Michael and Saint Raphael every day. The Saint Michael prayer is as follows:

> St. Michael the Archangel, defend us in battle.
> Be our defense against the wickedness and snares of
> the Devil.
> May God rebuke him, we humbly pray,
> and do thou, O Prince of the Heavenly host,
> by the power of God, thrust into Hell Satan,
> and all the evil spirits,
> who prowl about the world seeking the ruin of souls.
> Amen.

My prayer to Saint Raphael is as follows:

> Saint Raphael, please pray for me and my family so that
> we might fulfill our teaching and healing ministry.

It is also the tradition of the Catholic Church that each human has a "Guardian Angel." This is an Angel who is with us constantly and is available to help guide us on our path to Heaven. I will often ask my Guardian Angel to remind me to do something at a particular time. I am a little embarrassed that I don't utilize my Guardian Angel in a more meaningful fashion. But it is important to remember that your guardian Angel is, in fact, a Saint. And like any other Saint, your guardian Angel can be an intercessor to God for you when you have needs or wishes.

Our family has a couple of interesting stories regarding Guardian Angels. Let me tell you about the Angel who appeared at the wedding of my daughter Angela.

My son, Russell, age eleven, was an altar server at the wedding of Tim and Angela. After the ceremony my wife, Mary, mentioned that she saw Russell get very emotional during the ring ceremony. I didn't think too much about that; the entire family was somewhat emotional.

A couple of days later, however, when I was alone with Russell, he said, "Dad, I saw an Angel at the wedding. It was huge. It came down from the ceiling of the church, placed his hands over the rings during the ring ceremony, and then flew off into the ceiling."

The first thing I did was to check the wedding video taken during the ring ceremony. In that video the Angel was not visible to us, but you could see Russell's eyes following intently as the Angel descended from the ceiling, blessed Tim and Angela, and then left through the ceiling.

It wasn't until a month later that we got confirmation of the event from another source. Angela was talking to her friend from Binghamton, New York, who was unable to attend the wedding. Angela shared the Angel story. The friend responded, "Well, that makes sense. I sent my Guardian Angel over to bless your wedding!"

Well, needless to say, our family was happy to experience that blessing from God.

Another angel experience happened as follows. My wife, Mary, my son, Rob, and my youngest daughter, Heather, were riding in one of our clunker cars. Of note is that this car had a habit of stalling.

Rob was driving, Mary was in the front passenger seat, and Heather, age 6, was in the rear seat. The car had only two front doors, no rear doors. On their route they had to cross over a railroad track. As they attempted to drive over the track, you won't believe what happened next. The clunker car stalled directly on top of the track itself.

Suddenly there was a train coming towards them at seventy-five miles per hour. There was no time to react.

Inexplicably the stalled, powerless car moved smoothly forward, **_uphill_**, as the massive train screamed by only inches from the rear bumper. The engine of the car was still off!

What happened? To this day we think the experience was a message from God. He was telling us, ***"Thanks for your witness. Thanks for putting on your clunker's bumper the sticker with the words: 'Angels are protecting us!'"***

Our family has had some concrete experiences with the bad angels also (demons).

Most of you have heard the term "exorcism." This is when the demons gain so much control over a human being that the Catholic Church must get involved and, in the name of Jesus, take authority over the demons and command them to leave. I participated in the exorcism of a young man who was possessed by several demons. My role was minimal. I served on the support team and was one of the prayer intercessors and was also responsible for holding tightly one arm of the youngster to keep him from hurting himself or others.

A Catholic priest said the exorcism prayers in Latin while another very knowledgeable and experienced individual gave guidance to the exorcism team. Anyway, during the exorcism, the demon spoke to me through the possessed person and taunted me about a situation within my family that was known to me but to no one else in the room. I didn't respond, of course. But it was confirmation to me that we were indeed dealing with supernatural demonic forces. Further confirmation of the possession came at the conclusion of the exorcism ritual after all the demons were cast out. At that point the young man began to talk with us and it was apparent that he had no awareness of what had happened during the previous ninty minutes of tumultuous combat between the Latin speaking priest and the demon screaming to us from within him. The young man was rubbing his arms and trying to understand why they were bruised and sore where the team had restrained him.

It is important to note that the young man was not responsible for his condition. His adult caregivers had used their authority to dedicate him to Satan when he was very young. They had involved him in numerous Satanic rituals.

Bottom line: God is real! Angels are real! Demons are real! *Be aware!* That is urgent advice from your grandpa!

The Enemy - Basic Tactics

Let me briefly discuss some basic tactics used by the Enemy, Satan.

His primary tactic is to convince people that he does not exist. Or a variant of that theme accepted by many people is to believe that he does exist, but he is not bothering me. Wrong!

The Bible often refers to the battle against evil. In Ephesians Chapter 6, starting with Verse 10, Saint Paul writes:

> "Draw your strength from the Lord and from His mighty power. Put on the armor of God so that you may be able to stand firm against the tactics of the Devil. *For our struggle is not with flesh and blood* but with the principalities, with the powers, with the world rulers of this present darkness, with the *evil spirits* in the heavens."

Said more simply, Saint Paul is telling us that our earthly struggle is not with other humans, but with demonic forces led by Satan, the Devil. Note, however, that it is important to realize that the Devil does work through other people. They are often unwitting accomplices when he is tempting us to do something evil.

Now let us speak more about other tactics of the Devil.

I mentioned *possession*. This is extremely rare. In the case of possession, the Enemy has the power to completely take over a human. To deal with this, the Catholic Church requires that a Bishop be the one to make the decision to perform an Exorcism on a person. And the Bishop will only do that after the individual has had a psychiatric exam to confirm that it is a case of possession and not a case of pure mental illness.

What is a lot more common than possession is the case of *obsession*, *harassment*, or *temptation*.

Typically, *obsession* is when an individual is under heavy attack in a particular area of his or her life. Often this can be identified by addictions. People can be addicted to almost everything. The more common ones are: drugs, alcohol, smoking, pornography, food, power, and the list goes on. There are Christian ministries that address demonic activities that fall into this area. These ministries are referred to as *"Deliverance" ministries*. One well-known ministry that I know about is called *"Unbound Ministry"* which was started by Neal Lozano. My wife and I have attended a training session for this ministry.

An excellent summary of the methods involved are included in Neal's book entitled **"Unbound: A Practical Guide to Deliverance."**

Harassment is the tactic whereby you are attacked by an increased level of temptation focused on your weaknesses or by an increased level of painful circumstances such as the mean words from people.

Temptation is the tactic whereby the unseen enemy will whisper thoughts to your subconscious that, if acted upon, constitute a sin. These could be thoughts of revenge, lust, judgment, unforgiveness, hate, and so on. ***This is the most common tactic used by the Enemy.***

We can learn a lot about Satan by the names used in the Bible to reference him. The more common ones are as follows: Devil, Liar, Enemy, Dragon, Deceiver, Murderer, Adversary, Tempter, Beast, Accuser, Beelzebub, Evil One, Lucifer, Power of Darkness, Serpent, and Thief. I have one of my own that I will add: ***Evil Magician***.

The Enemy - His Successes

It is unsettling to see how successful the Enemy has been during the past 100 years. For starters, just consider the wars.

About 100 years ago, there was World War I. There were 17 million people killed. (Satan loves it when people kill other people.)

Then about 75 years ago, there was World War II. This was even worse than World War I. Over 50 million (50,000,000) people were killed.

There have been several wars since World War II, but let me get to current times. We now have abortion. This is a war against unborn babies. To me, this war is almost too personally painful to discuss. ***The tactic used by Satan to promote abortion explains why I call him the*** <u>***Evil Magician***</u>***.***

The way a magician works is that he distracts you with one hand while he does something with the other hand that you fail to notice. That is how he deceives so many of us humans. He gets everyone focused on the young mother who has just become pregnant and prevents your attention from focusing on the unborn baby. His solution: we need to prevent the mother from suffering with this unwanted circumstance.

Satan has been so successful in perpetuating this war that 60 million (60,000,000) people have been killed in the United States alone! Even now, for example, if you are an unborn child in the womb of a mother in New York City, you have less than a 50% chance of being born alive. If you have the condition known as Down Syndrome, then your chance of being born is less than 10%.

Lord God, have mercy on us! Forgive us! Forgive all of us who are a party to this evil, either actively or passively. And thank You, God, for sending my granddaughter, Felicity, to our family so that we are exposed to, and enlightened with, the love that You send us through her Down Syndrome condition!

The Evil Magician has succeeded in making abortion a political issue rather than a moral issue. Thus, rather that discuss whether abortion is good or evil, the discussion focuses on the "rights" of the mother to do what she wants "with her own body." This argument ignores the fact that there are TWO bodies involved. It also ignores the fact that none of us has our "own body." What we do have is a body ***loaned*** to us by God for this short time on earth. In case anyone has not noticed, we cannot take our body with us as we enter our eternal life.

Abby Johnson is a woman who became enlightened when she saw an actual abortion. Early in her life, when she was a young college-age woman, Abby had two abortions. At the time she procured her abortions, she didn't think too much about it. It didn't bother her. Eventually she went to work for ***Planned Parenthood*** to help other women who needed abortions. She was even recognized as "Employee of the Year." After eight years of working there in the office, she was asked to help in the operating room. When she did, the truth of what was happening shocked her to the core. She was horrified. For the first time, she also realized how her own abortions were affecting her mental health.

Abby now works full-time trying to save pregnant women from killing their own unborn babies and then living with the secret and the guilt for a lifetime. She is also trying to save the workers at Planned Parenthood who are participating in this genocide. God bless her! She has a ***book*** out called **Unplanned** which tells her dramatic story.

I personally believe that most young women who have abortions are completely unaware of the magnitude of their choice. It is highly probable that many of them are quite innocent, but have been sucked into a world-wide, evil, highly organized and efficient extermination process for human babies which makes the horrific Jewish Holocaust seem almost miniscule by comparison. This evil extermination process includes many components, including Planned Parenthood, the news media, politicians, social media, the medical profession, and countless other ***well-meaning*** individuals and groups who are being ***duped*** and ***unknowingly directed by the Evil Magician.***

Then once these pregnant women have participated in the holocaust of abortion, they are likely to discover the Truth eventually and then have to deal with a lifetime of regret and guilt.

I have included on the next page a graphic which highlights the logic behind the decision of the Catholic Church to define abortion as evil and the taking of a human life.

The graphic shows the development of the baby from conception through birth. If you look at the development, and start on the left side of the graphic which shows the moment of conception of the unborn baby and work your way to the right towards birth, ***you will note that there is no moment during the continuum of natural development that the unborn baby is somehow changed from "not human" to a "human."*** Before conception, an egg will always be just an egg; a sperm will always be just a sperm. But at the moment when the egg and sperm meet, a 46 chromosome human being is created. After conception, there is nothing to add to this new "being" besides nutrition. Thus, the Catholic Church naturally defines ***<u>conception</u> as the beginning of human life***, the beginning of a person, the beginning of a child of God. And this child of God has the God-given right to life!

Human development: conception to birth

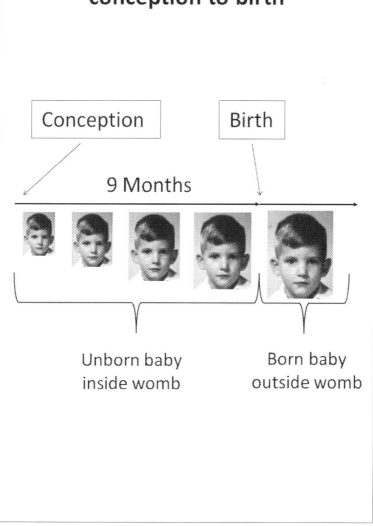

So what are some of the other successes of the Enemy in contemporary time? Well, the list is almost endless. But let me focus on the *"sexual revolution"* and the aftermath.

I was there in the 1960's when the sexual revolution started. It was in full swing during my college years. The motto of the revolutionaries: *"If it feels good, do it!"*

Those are the words every college student wants to hear. It was like telling everyone like myself, "You can eat two quarts of Haagen-Dazs every day. No problem."

A driving force behind this cultural revolution was the *Birth Control Pill* which became available in 1960. The Pill allowed people to engage in sex without causing pregnancy. Wow! To most people this was perceived to be the "freedom pill." Even many faithful married Catholics at the time were overjoyed. Pleasure without consequences. For single people, it was pleasure *without consequences or commitment*.

I was President of the Science Club at a Catholic College. Our club sponsored a debate about the morality of the birth control pill for contraception. I happened to be on the team that argued that it was wrong to use birth control pills. A good friend and a very holy person was on the team that took the opposing view. They argued that it was a good idea to use the birth control pill. At the time the Catholic Church had not determined the morality of using the Pill for contraception.

Only five years later Saint Pope Paul VI published a letter (*i.e.* *Encyclical*) called "Of Human Life" (a.k.a. *Humanae Vitae in Latin*). The letter re-affirmed the orthodox teaching of the Catholic Church regarding married love, responsible parenthood, and the continued rejection of most forms of artificial contraception. The letter flat-out rejected the use of the Pill as well as other forms of *artificial contraception* (e.g. condoms) which prevent conception during moments of marital union. The letter did, however, indicate that Catholics could use a technique called "Natural Family Planning."

This letter shocked some in the Catholic world. In fact, this letter from the Pope caused many to leave the Catholic Church. Even today, fifty years later, it causes many to disagree with the Truth as taught by the Church leaders. Earlier I mentioned an author named Christopher

West. He nearly left the Church over this issue before he became enlightened. He is now a best-selling Catholic author who specializes in explaining the Theology of the Body developed by Saint Pope John Paul II. *He can see the big picture and is dedicated to communicating that vision to all the faithful.* He is now able to recognize and describe the unhealthy spiritual junk food that distracts us on the road to the Eternal Banquet.

The junk pleasure food that weighs us down and sucks us into slavery includes, but is not limited to, the following: fornication, adultery, abortion, contraception, and pornography. For those of you new to this subject, *fornication* refers to sexual relations between two unmarried people; *adultery* is sexual relations between two people whereby at least one of them is married. A *Catholic Marriage* is defined as the Sacramental union of one man and one woman.

A spiritual junk food that serves as a deadly *appetizer* to the even more deadly food of fornication or adultery is *pornography.* Pornography.... Wow! Is Satan ever having a field day with this. It all starts with the healthy desire for communion, for intimacy. Then Satan, the Liar and Pervert, gets us to focus on the pleasure of physical actions and ignore the spiritual, intellectual, and emotional levels of intimacy. Devastating! By virtue of this addiction, human body parts and the viewing of them become our gods, our idols. This tactic is sucking the world into a giant cesspool of evil. We need some serious help to avoid this temptation.

What is the historic impact of people eating spiritual junk food from the dumpster? About 50% of marriages end in divorce. Many young people are not even bothering to get married; there is no commitment. Women are often treated as objects of pleasure; they are not treated as respected and valued partners in an exciting journey to the Eternal Banquet. Children are often viewed as a burden; they are not viewed as gifts from God that will give you eternal joy.

As I mentioned earlier, there is a blinking neon sign on the shiny attractive dumpster filled with spiritual junk food. Let me say more about the blinking neon sign. *The blinking neon sign is the Entertainment industry.* In particular, Satan uses television programs and movies to brainwash us with a ***perverted perspective*** of the world. Some key messages he sends via this medium is as follows:

- Fornication and adultery are fun and exciting; everyone is doing it
- Lying and deception is interesting (e.g. Survivor)
- Religious people are bigots
- Killing is justifiable
- Kids are smarter than parents
- Fathers have no vital role in family life
- There are no heroes
- Money is important
- Perversion is funny
- Power is important
- Winning is a meaningful goal
- Religion is obsolete
- Sarcasm is sophisticated
- Holiness is quaint

God, we need help! We, your children, need help to combat the relentless attack against us.

God *is* sending help. Let us talk about that.

The on-going help we, the children of God, have is our religion. In the following sections, we will learn more about the role of religion to fight the Enemy. We will also learn about our personal cross and the role of Mercy.

Following that we will discuss one of God's greatest gifts to us: Mary, the Blessed Virgin Mother; the Mother of Jesus Christ; our spiritual mother!

Defeating the Enemy - The Role of Religions

To describe what is happening in the spiritual war that is underway, consider the following analogy with respect to religions.

Every human being is in a boat or ship. The Christians are in a large naval fleet that is steaming rapidly towards a final confrontation with the naval forces of evil. The evil naval force is very powerful and very organized. It is led by Lucifer, the head demon, who is a fallen angel and has a superior intellect to humans.

The Christian naval fleet has an aircraft carrier with the Pope as the Captain. ***All faithful Catholics are on the aircraft carrier.*** The aircraft carrier is named "Ark of the Covenant." The non-Catholic Christians are in the destroyers and cruisers which are heading in the same direction as the aircraft carrier. Each of these smaller Christian ships are ready to engage the enemy and are using the battle plan, the Bible, to direct their actions.

Likewise, the humans on the Catholic aircraft carrier, led by the Pope, are using the Bible to direct their actions. These Catholics have an advantage, however. Since the enemy changes his strategy over time, the Pope can expand and adapt the basic plan in the Bible to the evolving situation based on real-time intelligence.

Naval fleets always have a fleet commander. The Pope is, in truth, the fleet commander for the Christian fleet, but is not recognized as such by the smaller supporting ships. Thus, the power of the entire naval fleet is compromised. Some of the smaller ships are beginning to drift away from the relative safety of the adjacent Christian ships.

In addition, the enemy is using submarines extensively. His tactic is to attack first the smaller Christian vessels that separate themselves from the main fleet. Many of these smaller vessels are badly damaged and are taking on water. They are in danger of sinking.

Even the Catholic aircraft carrier is badly damaged. The enemy has gained support among some Catholic officers. These corrupted individuals are attacking fellow passengers, both young and old, both overtly and covertly.

There are two other naval fleets heading in the same direction as the Christians: the Jewish Fleet and the Muslim Fleet. They have the same objective as the Christian Fleet, but are using a variation of the Bible battle plan. In addition, they do not accept the Pope as the commander who can coordinate all three fleets.

Now what about the atheists? What about the humans who do

not believe that God exists? Well, sad to say, they are the ones floating about completely alone in the huge ocean in a small dinghy. They are severely exposed in many ways. It is the mission of the people in the bigger ships to convince them to abandon their tiny, makeshift vessels and climb onto something more seaworthy before they are swallowed up in a huge wave or sunk by an enemy submarine.

So if the enemy is superior in intelligence to humans, how do the compromised forces of good overcome the organized and powerful forces of evil?

It is actually quite simple. We must take the role of David in his battle with Goliath. We need to rely on God to lead all His forces as we careen towards the final battle. He is the Ultimate Commander of all fleets: Jewish, Christian, and Muslim. Moreover, all of us humans must acquiesce now and acknowledge His sovereignty and pay attention to His commands.

For faithful Catholics the commands of God are very easy to hear and understand. We need only to pay attention to the Bible messages, the Pope and Bishops, and the Holy Spirit who speaks to each of us when we communicate in prayerful silence. Likewise, all other God-fearing humans must use everything provided to them by their religious leaders to hear and understand the living commands from God.

All humans who have faith in the Almighty know that the battle will be won! The only unknown is whether we, as individuals, will remain loyal to the Commander in Chief, God, and to our fellow soldiers. The ultimate reward for the loyal is Heaven. Praise God!

Carrying Our Personal Cross

In the Gospel of Matthew (16:24), Jesus said to his disciples,

"Whoever wishes to come after Me must deny himself, take up his cross, and follow Me."

Jesus is speaking to each one of us. We must take up our cross and fulfill our mission in life!

How do we do that? What is our cross?

Everyone has a cross. Some people have a huge cross; others have a tiny cross. Only God knows the size of our individual cross. I'll share with you my understanding of my personal cross. But before that, let me tell you a story about a friend of mine.

This friend was at a prayer meeting of sorts, and she felt compelled (by the Holy Spirit) to give to another woman, a stranger, this tiny cross she was carrying in her pocket. As she introduced herself and handed the gift of the tiny cross to the stranger, the stranger shrieked in surprise and dismay. It turns out the recipient had just been praying to God and complaining about the huge cross she was being asked to carry.

Based on that example, it would be hard to accuse God of not having a sense of humor. I'm sure there were numerous Angels hovering nearby chuckling along with our Heavenly Father.

So with that as a backdrop, I'll share what I perceive to be my cross. And I'll say in advance that, in the scheme of things, it is quite small.

A significant piece of my personal cross is dictated by circumstances at birth. In my case, I was born in the United States in the twentieth century to a married couple, one of whom was a faithful Catholic (my mom). We were not poor; nor were we rich. Physically I was gifted with above average intelligence as it relates to scholarly success. My physical handicaps included color blindness, environmental allergies and slight asthma. The allergies caused significant discomfort to me as I grew up on a farm. But all-in-all my physical cross is quite small.

My emotional cross is also relatively quite small, but does have an impact on my life. There were some memorable events which affected me.

When I was about five years old, I ate too much corn at dinner and started complaining about the pain. My mom was giving me some sympathy, but my dad took a different approach. He went into the kitchen and grabbed a huge butcher knife. He approached me, brandished the knife, and said, "I will cut open your stomach and get the corn out. Okay?"

Needless to say, I told him that my stomach didn't hurt any more.

That experience gave me a message: don't express your feelings, especially if they are painful.

Another set of experiences which had an impact on my emotional development in my youth was when my dad would regularly come home drunk late at night. During this period of my life I was in the range of seven to ten years old. My mom and dad would start verbally fighting. My sister, Mary Jean, four years older than me, would engage every time in an attempt to resolve the situation. When that failed, she would call upstairs to me, where I was lying in my bed trying to ignore the shouting. "Bob, come down here now. Dad is going to kill mom!"

Sometimes I would come to help my sister defuse the situation. But as a general rule I would just cover my head with my blanket and try to "sleep." Then in the morning I would awake and hope there were no dead bodies in the living room. *(It is important to note that my dad was baptized into the Catholic Church the week before he died at age 50!)*

As a result of these "family fight" experiences, my normal reaction to a conflict situation is to go to bed, wrap my head in a pillow, and let sleep take to me to the safe place of unconsciousness. If retreat is not possible, then my survival emotions kick in and I get prepared to "fight to the death!"

This cross of emotional programming carries on in our lives. I recall during a session with a psychologist I was asked about some situation with one of my children. She said, "How does that make you feel?"

I responded in all seriousness, "I don't understand the question."

She quipped, "Does it make you happy, sad, mad, or glad?"

I answered, "None of those."

It turns out that I was over fifty years old and didn't have a conscious awareness of my feelings. When you are in survival mode, you don't have the luxury of having feelings.

With emotional programming like mine, the spirit of FEAR becomes a predominant driving force in one's life. The unconscious solution: avoid conflict; avoid risk; avoid pain; avoid being vulnerable. Avoid people!

My cross is not very unique. Almost every human can relate to my cross. Everyone has been hurt by someone they trusted... and some hurt very badly.

Okay, so what?

We need to move on. We need to FORGIVE the people who hurt us. They didn't know any better. They were wounded by someone they trusted! That's the way it works. That's the way life is set up. Actually, the Church has a name for it: Original Sin!

Once we have forgiven everyone who has hurt us, including ourselves, then we must do what Jesus says,

> *"If anyone wishes to come after Me, he must deny himself and take up his cross <u>daily</u> and follow Me."*
> (Luke 9:23).

As it turns out, you need a personal cross to fulfill your mission. As a disciple of Jesus Christ, you have a mission to be life-giving bread for others (John 21:15-17). And Jesus knows that *bread has to be <u>broken</u> (by your cross) to be eaten by others....*

So God will arrange your life and give you a cross designed specifically for you so that you will be broken!... Think about that for a moment.... And be grateful.

Mercy: A Powerful Spiritual Weapon

I gained some insight about mercy from one particularly difficult experience with a teenager. My son, Russell, became old enough to get a driver's license. However, based on some of his disobedience to the family rules, I told him that he could not get his license as originally scheduled. Naturally, he was devastated.

Three days later, on his sixteenth birthday, his older sister, Heidi, called me from college. She told me about the dream/vision she had about Russell. The net of the dream is that he needed to feel loved.

Based on what I considered as a sign from God, I changed my decision and told Russell that he could get his driver's license immediately. Obviously, he was thrilled.

The insight I gained from this experience is as follows:

1. ***Mercy must happen NOW***
2. ***It cannot be negotiated or contracted, or it is not mercy***
3. ***Mercy is a gift***
4. ***God gives me mercy without conditions***
5. ***God trusts me without conditions***

Wow! For the first time I understood the difference between the "Law" as taught in the Old Testament of the Bible and the NEW "Law of Love" as taught by Jesus. The difference was profound.

We are programmed from birth with **conditional love**: if you obey I will give you my approval (and approval is perceived as "love"). Thus, it is nearly impossible for us to understand that God's approval and acceptance of us does NOT depend on us being "good" and obeying His rules.

God's mercy is available to us for the taking. The Enemy will appeal to your programming and attempt to convince you that you are not worthy of God's love. You must reject this diabolical lie!

Jesus is Mercy personified. Accept this unconditional gift from your Father in Heaven. Win the spiritual battle; win the spiritual war!

God's mercy is at work and affecting us all the time. Often we are unaware of how often we "dodge a bullet." At other times, we become aware. I'll give some examples.

I was working for IBM in Oakland, California and was scheduled to attend a school for new managers in Southbury, Connecticut. As I flew cross-country to attend the class, I started to realize that something was going on with my body. I felt nauseous and I was having sharp pains in my abdomen. I began to feel weaker and weaker.

The plane landed in Hartford. A limo had been arranged. I was taken to the motel reserved for class attendees. Upon arrival in my room, my symptoms became more acute. One minute I was vomiting, the next I was going to the bathroom. I finally became so weak that I was fearful of passing out.

I called the front desk and had them order an ambulance. The first responders arrived. They helped me onto a gurney and loaded me into the ambulance. A young man was tending to me. I'll never forget the look on his face when he took my blood pressure. His eyes became huge and completely round. It turns out that I had been bleeding internally all day and half my blood was gone. I was in a critical state.

They rushed me to the hospital in Waterbury. There they started a blood transfusion to replace my lost blood. They were having a problem, however. I was losing about as much blood as they were adding. They decided they needed to do surgery the next morning to find out where I was bleeding and fix the problem.

As I lie in bed that evening thinking about the operation that was planned for early the next morning, I suddenly felt a sense of well-being and peace. I sensed that I was not bleeding anymore. It was exactly midnight. I felt great!

The next morning two members of the hospital staff came to wheel me to the operating room. I told them that I was healed. I told them that I was not bleeding anymore. They ignored me. They probably thought I was making a desperate attempt to avoid exploratory surgery.

Finally I was in the surgery prep room and the nurses were completing the final checklist for my surgery. The surgeon walked in, looked at what was happening with my stomach pump, and exclaimed, "He's not bleeding anymore!"

My reaction: "Yes!"

Later that day I had a phone conversation with Mary. It turns out that my bleeding stopped at the exact moment my wife and her friends were in California praying for my healing (at 9 p.m. Pacific time). Praise God!

Now God's miracles are not confined to one dimension. The blood I received in Waterbury Hospital was tainted. As a result, I was infected with the Hepatitis C virus, which destroys the liver over time.

This was a blessing in disguise, as they say. Or as I would say, everything that happens is a gift from God. As a result of my liver deteriorating, I was required to maintain a "no alcohol" regimen. This kept me from becoming an alcoholic, like my father. Many years later, as my liver damage was on the verge of becoming seriously problematic, researchers created a miracle drug to combat Hep C. I was able to take this drug. After three months of treatment there was no sign of the Hepatitis C virus in my system.

A few years after my internal bleeding incident, Mary had an opportunity to experience God's mercy. Shortly after our family moved from California to New York state, the doctors discovered that she had a rapidly growing tumor inside one of her ribs. At the time, all of our nine kids had been born.

We were able to connect with a doctor and get an appointment for surgery at the Sloan Kettering Cancer Center in New York City. We were very concerned that the tumor was cancerous.

Prior to the surgery we participated in a healing Mass at Saint Mary's Church in Katonah, New York. The priest prayed over Mary and she "rested in the Spirit." As she was lying on the floor, she felt heat in the area of the tumor. As a result, our fear turned to optimism. Perhaps she was going to be okay.

She had the surgery shortly thereafter. We were thrilled and relieved to be told that the tumor was NOT cancerous! Praise God!

I am also aware of some instances where God intervened with my children.

My daughter, Nichole, was scheduled to work in Manhattan on September 11, 2001. As she neared the city, she providentially saw the initial smoke from the World Trade Towers caused by the first terrorist attack. She reversed her route in time to avoid being a victim of the largest terrorist attack against America.

My daughter, Marianne, was moved by the Spirit to spend time with an order of religious sisters who had an orphanage in Peru for handicapped children. It was necessary for her to resign from her special education teaching position in Newtown, Connecticut to respond to God's will and discern the alternative vocation.

God was protecting her. During her absence from her school, which was Sandy Hook Elementary, a troubled young man invaded the school and killed 26 people.

Marianne is again teaching in the Newtown school district, in a different school. Even though she was not present when the shooting occurred, she has been traumatized. Many of the victims were close associates. Also, the previous year she was the teacher for two of the students who were killed.

There are no accidents. God has a plan for Marianne and experiences such as this are part of that plan. She has tremendous compassion. She has extensive experience in spiritual warfare. Marianne, like the rest of us, is being prepared for the future as the battle intensifies.

There is another experience Mary and I had which is interesting. Here is what happened.

Mary had two miscarriages and they were quite traumatic for her. Then we heard about a ministry called ***Project Rachel***. The purpose of Project Rachel is to facilitate healing for women after an abortion or a miscarriage. We attended. It was very therapeutic. During one part of the session the parents pray to discern the name of the baby who is now in Heaven. According to one unofficial tradition it is believed that the name of every child is determined by God at conception, and we humans instinctively assign that name upon birth. So we prayed. The names that came to Mary for the two unborn children were Peter and Paul.

A few years later, Mary and I participated in the annual March for Life in Washington, DC. I chose to bring with me a painting of a crucified, unborn baby. An image of that painting follows. To me the image shows an unborn baby who is a member of the Mystical Body of Christ and who is being crucified by people who are oblivious to the consequences of their actions. In other words, history is being repeated: over 2000 years ago we crucified Jesus; now we are all crucifying a living, unborn, baby Jesus countless times every day.

Before the march itself began, I held the image over my head and walked into a group of Pro-Choice activists. Suddenly I was shouting out the following words, ***"God is pro-choice! You can choose good, or you can choose evil!"*** The Holy Spirit was speaking through me, ***with power!***

Instantly I was attacked by what seemed to me to be people consumed by demonic forces. They were trying to reach the image and destroy it. They were all around me. They were hitting me and pulling on my arms. My mind became filled with one thought: "This may be the day I die!" There was no emotion associated with that thought: no fear; no joy. There was just the acknowledgement of an objective reality.

Then I felt an unseen force literally eject me from the crazed group. I was able to escape. Mary had been watching from nearby. She led me to a safe place where we tried to collect ourselves and lick our wounds, so to speak.

Two men approached us. They asked, "What can we do to help?" We responded, "We are okay now. What are your names?"

One responded, "My name is Peter."

The other man said, "My name is Paul."

Mary and I both felt goose-bumps on our arms as we realized that, perhaps, we were encountering our two deceased (unborn) sons who had appeared in the flesh to give us consolation. Who knows?

In any case, we know that our unborn sons, Peter and Paul, will be there to greet us when we arrive at the Pearly Gates.

Secrets: Mine and Yours

Okay, I have kept a secret for nearly seventy years. And I think that God wants me to share it now for your benefit. It's not something I would share if I didn't think it was God's will. In fact, I kept waiting for my family proofreaders to tell me to take it out. That didn't happen.

Before I tell the story, I need to give you a warning. When Jesus was in the desert and tempted by the devil, He said, "Do not put the Lord your God to the test" (Luke 4:12). So DO NOT do something as stupid as I did; you can't expect God to bail YOU out if He knows you are doing it merely to test Him.

When I was about five years old, I did something without giving it any thought. I *now* believe that I killed my one-year-old sister, Betty, and then God brought her back to life. However, I didn't know at that time what really happened. I think I understand it now. Let me explain the situation.

It was summer on the farm. My baby sister, Betty, was sleeping on my parents' bed. My mom had to go outside for a short time and help my dad. My mom told me to watch Betty so that she didn't roll off and get hurt.

So I took up my post. Betty was lying there peacefully on her back. She was beautiful. She was breathing softly. She had an angelic look on her face. There was a slight breeze coming through the open window on the east side of the room.

Suddenly I noticed the pillow lying beside her. Without giving it any thought, I picked up the pillow and placed it on her face. I held the pillow on her face until she stopped squirming. Then I removed it.

At the time I don't think I understood death and how it worked. I just knew that my sister was lying there and not breathing. I was responsible.

Why did I do it? To this day, I really don't know what motivated me. I was in the moment. Prior to inadvertently suffocating my sister, I had no ill feelings towards her. She was my sister. She was beautiful. Perhaps, like many five-year-old kids, I just did something without thinking. It was as if I was subconsciously conducting a science experiment.

But now my sister was just lying there. She was not moving. She was not breathing. I had no plan or concept of how to deal with the situation.

After a couple of minutes she suddenly started breathing again... and so did I. I had no concept of the potential consequences of my actions. I was just being me; I was just being a five-year-old.

Well, no problem. She was breathing again. No one knew. There was no reason to tell anyone. She obviously had not died, right?

Fast forward sixty-five years. During a recent visit with my sister, Betty, she said to me, "Bob, I had a vivid dream last night. I dreamt you suffocated me with a pillow when I was a baby. It was so realistic! In the dream I had an out-of-body experience and watched you from above as you reacted after I died. Then suddenly I was back in my body."

I was flabbergasted. This event had happened nearly a lifetime earlier. There were only two people who knew my secret: me and my one-year-old sister, Betty. Wow! A feeling of guilt came over me. I was found out.

I have reflected on that experience and wondered what God was telling me now. He could have let me go on blissfully in my life, never knowing that He apparently raised someone from the dead to keep me from feeling a lifetime of guilt. I cannot imagine how I would have dealt with Betty's death knowing that I was the cause. Every day I would ask myself, "Should I tell someone? Who? Why? What was I thinking? How could I be so stupid?" I would have been trapped in a living hell. The pain would have been unbearable.

I think the reason God gave me that experience is to give consolation and relief to women who have had an abortion. If you have had an abortion, stick with me as I explain.

Like me, you made a decision to abort without understanding the consequences. Your life as you knew it was being threatened, and you were acting on your instinct to survive. The Evil Magician, who has many well-meaning human helpers, kept your mind focused on the "solution" to your pain, and kept your mind off the unborn baby. You reacted. Problem solved.

But as the Enemy knows, now you have a bigger problem. Over time you began to realize the magnitude of your thoughtless action. Guilt and regret crept into your subconscious. From that point on the natural progression is to become increasingly ill emotionally.

My hope is that you are ready to receive God's mercy now. If you followed the concepts in this book up to this point, let me explain.

I said, "There are no accidents; everything that comes to you is from God's Providence." Everything is therefore good that God brings to you. It is part of His plan, which we are incapable of comprehending. Even "bad" things from Satan are part of God's plan: just read the Book of Job in the Old Testament. Satan can only attack you within the constraints given to him by God.

Every well-known spiritual writer is in agreement with me: <u>everything that comes to you is from God and is good; it is Divine Providence even if it comes from a secondary source such as Satan or another person.</u>

What must be true for <u>you</u>, is then also true for <u>everyone else</u>. There are no accidents; everything that comes from God, directly or indirectly, is good.

That means that your unborn baby, a legitimate person in God's eyes, a person God has already named, received a gift from God as a result of your abortion. Your child was taken instantly taken into God's arms. Wow!

Why?... Why do some kids only two-years-old die? Why do some people live to 100 years of age? Why? Why? Why?

We don't know the mind of God. We do know He sent His only son to die a painful death on the cross to facilitate us joining Him in Heaven.

Okay, so if your baby is fine, what's the problem?

Here is the deal. Your baby is fine, *but you are not fine* until you rush into the arms of your loving Father and ask for forgiveness. For Catholics, your Father, your Papa, your Daddy, is waiting in the confessional, pacing the floor, waiting for you to *humble yourself* and *come home!* If you are not a Catholic, then you should reconcile with God in a manner consistent with your faith.

I also suggest you check out Project Rachel or other ministry that supports post-abortive trauma suffered by women.

God's name is Mercy! You are His creation. Reconcile now!

If abortion is not your secret, then be willing to acknowledge other serious errors you are keeping secret and rush to Confession now. Your Merciful Papa is waiting. Jettison your secrets! Throw them overboard! Lighten your load! *Claim your freedom! The time is now!*

Now let's discuss one of God's greatest gifts to us: Mary, the Blessed Virgin Mother; the Mother of Jesus Christ; our spiritual mother!

Mary is our Spiritual Mother

Why do Catholics believe that Mary of Nazareth is our spiritual mother? Because of what is said in the Bible. Consider the following exchange between Jesus and His mother as He was dying on the cross. Saint John the Evangelist (the disciple whom Jesus loved) was present also.

> When Jesus saw His mother and the disciple there whom He loved (John), He said to His mother, "Woman, behold, your son." Then He said to the disciple (John), "Behold your mother." And from that hour the disciple took her into his home. (John 19:26-27)

It is the teaching of our Catholic faith that when Jesus says "Woman, behold your son" He is signifying that Mary is to be the mother of ALL sons (and daughters) of God the Father. Likewise, when Jesus says to John "Behold your mother," He is telling John (and all children of God) that Mary is to be viewed as their spiritual mother!

Wow! Wonderful! What a gift to us from Jesus.

Now this does NOT mean that Mary is God, or is in any way divine. Rather it means that she has a special role in the plan of salvation. Her role is to lead us to Jesus by telling us, as she did the servants at the wedding in Cana when the wine ran out, "Do whatever He tells you."

The role of Mary, our spiritual mother, is to constantly remind us to do what Jesus tells us as written in the Bible. In addition, since she is the human mother of Jesus, she has a special relationship with Jesus, as well as God the Father and God the Holy Spirit. Thus Catholics believe that, like every other Saint in Heaven, she can intercede for us to God and help us in our quest for Heaven.

Mary is the Woman Clothed with the Sun

According to the ancient Biblical prophecy contained in the Book of Revelation, Chapter 12, the forces of good and evil are engaged in a cosmic war. The forces of good are led by "the Woman clothed with the sun, with the moon under her feet, and on her head a crown of twelve stars." The forces of evil are led by a "huge red dragon."

In the next section of this book, I included a copy of the only image of Mary that God has created and given us. It is the image that exists on the cloak of the Mexican Saint Juan Diego. Mary is known by the name of "Our Lady of Guadalupe" in the context of that apparition.

The "huge Red Dragon" is obviously another name for Satan.

While the language used to describe the cosmic spiritual war uses a lot of symbolism, the message is clear: the war is real; the war is deadly; and our Mother will lead the loyal followers of Jesus to victory!

Mary is the Ark of the Covenant

In Christianity, Mary, the Mother of God, is sometimes referred to as the Ark of the Covenant. This is very insightful when you reflect on the analogy.

First of all, there was the Ark that Noah built to save humanity from the flood that came to cleanse the earth from evil.

Secondly, there was the Ark of the Covenant that was carried by the Jewish People on their journey to the Promised Land. Contained in that Ark were the Ten Commandments from God and the Jewish Scriptures (i.e. the Old Testament of the Bible).

Now reflect on the role of Mary in the Divine plan of salvation. She is the mother of Jesus. In the Bible (Book of John) Jesus is referred to as "the Word." Thus, like the Jewish Ark, Mary was the receptacle of the Word of God.

Continuing that reflection about the role of Mary in the Divine plan of salvation, consider that she is the Ark that God sent us to keep us from drowning in the flood of evil that is covering the earth right now. Wow! Cool!

Our Spiritual Mother is Guiding us Now!

Our Mom comes to the rescue! Yes, it is quite remarkable. Our spiritual mother, the Blessed Virgin Mary, has been coming to earth regularly to give us guidance and support in these latter days. She is often seen by regular people in a vision. These visions are called *apparitions*. Many of these sightings have been officially approved by the leaders of the Catholic Church. Some are still under investigation. There are also some apparitions that were determined to be hoaxes and are condemned by the Catholic Church.

There are eight apparitions that I would like to mention here. I have had the opportunity to visit the sites of seven of them.

- 1531. Our Lady of Guadalupe.
- 1830. Our Lady of the Miraculous Medal.
- 1858. Our Lady of Lourdes.
- 1879. Our Lady of Knock.
- 1917. Our Lady of Fatima.
- 1961. Our Lady of Mount Carmel at Garabandal.
- 1981. Our Lady of Kibeho in Rwanda.
- 1981. Our Lady Queen of Peace at Medjugorje.

Six of these apparitions have been officially approved. The apparitions at Garabandal have not been officially approved. The visions at Medjugorje are under investigation and are the most dramatic in many ways which I will address. As far as church approval, it is common that any apparition will not be approved by the Church while they are still happening. This is for obvious reasons. And thus, despite the fact that the Medjugorje apparitions have occurred for over 35 years, it is unlikely the church will approve them as long as the visionaries are still receiving apparitions.

So what are the messages that God has asked the Blessed Virgin Mary to deliver? Let's talk briefly about each apparition and its impact.

Our Lady of Guadalupe

The Blessed Virgin Mary appeared to an illiterate farmer in Mexico in the year 1531. The impact of this visit by our Mother is almost incomprehensible. Millions of inhabitants of Mexico and the surrounding countries were converted to Catholicism as a result of this appearance and the permanent gift she left.

It all started on the morning of December 9, 1531. A native Mexican peasant named Juan Diego saw a vision of a maiden at a place called the Hill of Tepeyac, near Mexico City. The maiden identified herself as the Virgin Mary, Mother of the true God, and asked Juan to tell the Archbishop that a church should be built at that site in her honor. She spoke to Juan Diego in his native Aztec language.

Juan Diego promptly contacted the Archbishop of Mexico City to tell him what happened. The skeptical Archbishop did not accept the idea.

Then the Virgin Mary visited Juan Diego again and insisted that her request to the Archbishop be carried out. So the obedient Juan Diego again contacted the Archbishop to relay the message. This time the Archbishop told Juan to request from the Blessed Mother a sign as a confirmation of her message to him.

So on Tuesday, December 12, 1531, the Blessed Mother again appeared to Juan Diego. That morning Juan Diego was actually trying to avoid the Blessed Mother because his uncle had fallen sick and was on his deathbed. He went around the other side of the hill and was on his way to get a priest to administer Last Rites. The Virgin Mary intercepted Juan and chided him. She said, "Am I not here, I who am your mother?" She went on to assure Juan that his uncle had now recovered and that he need not worry about that. She went on to tell Juan to gather flowers on the top of the hill to bring to the Archbishop to respond to his request for a sign.

Normally no flowers would be growing on this hill since it was December. But Juan followed her instructions and, to his shock, found Castilian roses, not native to Mexico, blooming there. Juan, with the help of the Blessed Mother, arranged the flowers in his tilma (cloak), and proceeded down the hill to meet the Archbishop. Castilian roses were a favorite of the Archbishop who was a native of Spain.

Upon meeting the Archbishop, Juan Diego opened his cloak and showed the roses to the Archbishop. But the startled Archbishop was staring at something beyond belief. It was not the roses. There was an image of the Blessed Virgin Mary somehow miraculously imprinted on the cloak, or tilma, of Juan Diego. The actual image seen by the Archbishop is shown on the next page.

Image Courtesy of https://en.wikipedia.org/wiki/
Our_Lady_of_Guadalupe#/media/File:Virgen_de_guadalupe1.jpg

You may have heard the term "a picture is worth a thousand words." In the case of this image, a picture is worth millions of words. It is beyond our comprehension to understand what was communicated with one picture. Let me explain.

The first message is that it was an obvious miracle. This confirmed that, in fact, the Blessed Virgin Mary had visited Earth. Secondly, she wanted the Archbishop to build a church or chapel on the hill. She did not ask if it was practical or if he had enough money. She just issued the order knowing that, if he was obedient, the providence of God would take care of the rest.

But the real message was to the indigenous people of Mexico: the native Indians. At the time they were essentially pagan and were offering human sacrifices to their "gods." They were killing some of their children because that is what they thought their gods were demanding. They believed that they needed to appease these pagan gods, including the sun god and the moon god.

The Blessed Mother is shown in the image as a pregnant native Indian of royal blood. She is standing on the crescent moon and in front of the sun. The message is that her power and the authority that she represents is greater than the sun or the moon. Furthermore, by being pregnant, she shows that the children, both born and unborn, are precious and are also members of the Royal Family. Wow!

There are numerous other messages represented by this image which I won't recount here. But there is tremendous material available in this regard.

The end result is that you will see literally thousands of these images in Mexico and other countries where there are people of Mexican descent. They understand the messages. They understand that Mary is their Mother. And those who believe in the apparition understand the sanctity of human life both before and after birth. There is a world-wide Catholic Feast Day on December 12th of every year to honor this holy event.

And the miracle is still with us! The 500-year-old Tilma is hanging in the church that was built to satisfy the request of the Blessed Virgin Mary. The church is called the Basilica of Our Lady of Guadalupe. Over 10 million pilgrims visit this church every year.

The Tilma has not deteriorated. The image was not created by any form of paint as would be done if created by humans. It is scientifically inexplicable. It has even survived a bombing attempt.

My wife, Mary, and I saw the actual image during a pilgrimage in 1989. Thank You, God! Thank you Blessed Virgin Mary! Thank you Our Lady of Guadalupe.

Our Lady of the Miraculous Medal.

In November of 1830 in Paris, France, the Blessed Virgin Mary appeared to Saint Catherine Laboure. The apparitions occurred in the convent located on the Rue Du Bac where Saint Catherine lived as a Catholic nun. During the most significant apparition the Blessed Virgin Mary asked that a medallion be made according to a design that she dictated. Ultimately that design came to be known as the Miraculous Medal. The front of the medal displays an image of the Virgin as she appeared to Saint Catherine. The design on the reverse of the medal includes the letter M and a cross. This is a plain cross with an M underneath the right hand bar to signify the Blessed Virgin standing at the foot of the cross while Jesus was being crucified. Beneath the M are the hearts of Jesus and Mary, the one crowned with thorns, the other pierced with a sword. Our Lady said that, "All who wear this medal will receive great graces." An image of the medal is shown below.

The Miraculous Medal

Front   Back

*Image courtesy of https://en.wikipedia.org/wiki/
Miraculous_Medal#/media/File:Miraculous_medal.jpg*

The words in French on the front of the Medal say, "O Mary, conceived without sin, pray for us who have recourse to thee." Mary is shown standing on the Earth with rays of graces flowing from her hands to the faithful. Under her heel is the Serpent, Satan. Make special note of the words Our Lady gave to Saint Catherine: "...conceived without sin...." You will understand more fully the significance of this phrase when you read about the apparitions at Lourdes that take place twenty-eight years later.

The body of Saint Catherine is in the chapel of that convent today, almost 200 years later. Her body is incorrupt. She is resting in a glass case for all to see.

During a conversation that Saint Catherine had with our Blessed Mother in July of 1830, prior to her being given the image of the Miraculous Medal in November, she had another vision. Our Lady said, "The times are very evil. Sorrows will befall France; the throne will be overturned. ... But come to the foot of the altar. There graces will be shed upon all, great and small, who ask for them." During the same two hour conversation, Our Lady said that another community would ask to be united to the order of Saint Catherine. She was referring to Mother Seton's Sisters from Emmitsburg, Maryland, who petitioned for union and were admitted in 1849.

The impact on the world of the apparitions in France by the Blessed Virgin Mary is significant. The apparitions gave hope to the world then; and they give hope now. Hundreds of thousands of people in the world today wear a Miraculous Medal.

The following is my personal story about the Miraculous Medal I wear constantly.

As I mentioned earlier in this book, a year after I made the primal decision to commit to Jesus 100%, I made a decision to consecrate myself to Jesus through the Blessed Virgin Mary. I choose in advance the special day of December 8, 1992, the Feast of the Immaculate Conception, to say my final prayer of consecration. So on November 5th, thirty-three days prior to my predetermined consecration day, I started the daily prayers of preparation.

Well, God had a special gift for me. A couple of days after November

5th, for the first time ever, my job at IBM required me to travel to Paris on business. And, of course, since there are no accidents, I would be in Paris (working) on December 8th, with plans to fly to Milan, Italy, the next day.

To complete the miraculous sequence of events planned by God, I finished my work in Paris on the 7th, a day early. So out of respect for my work responsibilities, I dutifully contacted my travel agent and tried to rebook a flight to Milan for the 8th. Guess what? All flights from Paris to Milan were completely booked on the 8th due to a soccer tournament in Milan. Wow! I had no choice but to stay in Paris on the 8th, which gave me the opportunity to spend the entire day in the chapel at the Rue Du Bac!

What a day! I prayed a lot. I thanked God a lot. It was on that momentous day that I consecrated myself to Jesus through the Blessed Virgin Mary. Ever since that commitment twenty-five years ago I have worn a Miraculous Medal around my neck day and night.

As I left the Chapel that evening, a vagrant approached me and asked for money. I had no choice but to ask, "How much do you want?" Based on my commitment to God, if he had said, "Everything you own," I would have given it to him. I have to admit that I was more than a little relieved when he specified a modest amount.

As I explained in an earlier part of this book, when I had the opportunity to personally meet Saint Pope John Paul II in Rome less than two months later in January of 1993, he saw my Miraculous Medal and responded by presenting a Rosary to me and a Rosary to my wife, Mary. Wow! It turns out he has a special devotion to the Blessed Virgin Mary also. In fact, this Pope is convinced that it was our Blessed Mother who saved him from the assassin's bullet on May 13, 1981. I will explain more about that when I discuss the apparitions at Fatima.

If you are interested in consecrating yourself to Jesus through our Blessed Mother, there is a new book out which is based on the approach established by Saint Louis de Monfort, but is an updated and simplified version of the classic approach described in his book entitled **True Devotion**. The new book is entitled **33 Days to Morning Glory** by Michael E. Gaitley.

Obviously I would highly recommend the Consecration. But pray to God and let Him pick the right time for you. And don't forget, the Primal Decision that I described needs to be made first.

Our Lady of Lourdes

In the year 1858 a 14-year-old shepherd girl who lived near the town of Lourdes in France, Saint Bernadette Soubirous, was out gathering firewood in the countryside. The Blessed Virgin Mary appeared to her, but did not initially disclose who she was. When Bernadette reported this to her parents and to the local pastor, her story was met with skepticism. After the first two apparitions the impatient Catholic pastor told Bernadette to ask the lady to identify herself. Bernadette did ask during the apparitions that followed, but did not receive the answer at first.

The sixteenth apparition was very special, however. It took place on March 25, 1858. That day, when Bernadette again asked the Lady to identify her name, she did respond. *Our Lady said, "I am the Immaculate Conception."*

When Bernadette related this to her pastor, he was shocked. The doctrine of the Immaculate Conception had been established only 4 years earlier, on December 8, 1854, by the Catholic Church. *The doctrine essentially said that the Mother of Jesus, the Blessed Virgin Mary, had been preserved from Original Sin by God. This grace and privilege from Almighty God indicates that Mary is uniquely qualified for her role as the Mother of all mankind.*

There was obviously no way that Bernadette knew anything about this doctrine, or even understood it. This convinced the pastor that what Bernadette said was true.

Bernadette had eighteen visions in all. One of the results was that Bernadette followed the directive of the Blessed Mother and uncovered an underground spring which has healing powers for the faithful.

In other visions the Blessed Mother directed Bernadette to tell the local pastor that she wanted a chapel to be built on the site and that people should come in procession to the chapel. The chapel was built.

Years later a huge underground Basilica was added to accommodate the millions of visitors to the site.

How did the Lourdes apparitions impact the world? It seems obvious that the Doctrine of the Immaculate Conception instituted by Pope Pius IX would have been lost in headquarters documents and ignored if Our Lady had not appeared at Lourdes and ***dramatically publicized her unique and ongoing role in the divine plan of salvation.***

Lourdes is currently a major shrine for the Catholic Church. Every year there are six million people who make a pilgrimage to Lourdes with the intent of asking the Lord for healing. Numerous physical healings take place there. And whether or not one receives a physical healing, everyone who visits Lourdes can walk away with a mental or spiritual healing. It is a fantastic place to spend time with our Lord and His Mother.

Every evening at Lourdes the pilgrims walk in prayerful procession to the chapel. Everyone prays the Rosary in unison. The procession is led by a large statue of Our Lady.

My wife and I were blessed to have the opportunity to visit the Lourdes shrine in September of 2012. We were excited to join with the hundreds of joyful pilgrims in the daily procession. It was Heavenly!

Our Lady of Knock

On August 21, 1879, in Ireland at the Knock parish church, our Lady appeared above the roof. With her was Saint Joseph and Saint John the Evangelist. In addition, in the vision was a plain altar with the cross and a lamb with adoring Angels. The two hour apparition was seen by fifteen people whose ages range from six to seventy-five years and included men, women, and children. There have been numerous physical cures attributed to Knock following the apparition.

The message from our Lady was not given in words, but in the vision itself. She appears to be acting in her role as Queen of Heaven and interceding to God the Father for her children through the sacrifice of her son, Jesus.

About 1.5 million people make a pilgrimage to Knock every year.

My wife and I had the opportunity to visit this shrine in the Spring of 2014.

Our Lady of Fatima

In 1917 the Blessed Virgin Mary appeared to three shepherd children ages seven to ten in Fatima, Portugal. There were six apparitions, one a month, starting on May 13 and concluding on October 13. The children's names are Lucia, Francisco, and Jacinta. The messages emphasized the need to pray constantly, do sacrifices for our sins and the sins of others, and give devotion to the Immaculate Heart of Mary.

Fatima Visionaries

Lucia, Francisco, Jacinta

The following gives some highlights of the apparitions.

- Prior to the apparitions of Our Lady, in the year 1916, an Angel appeared three times to the children. He called himself the Angel of Peace. He explained that the children were to pray and make sacrifices. Lucia asked, "How?" The Angel said, "Offer up everything within your power as a sacrifice to the Lord in reparation for the sins by which He is so much offended and of supplication for the conversion of sinners. Thus bring peace upon your country. I am the Guardian Angel of Portugal. More than all else, accept and bear with resignation the sufferings that God may send you." During one apparition the Angel gave the children Holy Communion.

- May 13, 1917. Our Lady appeared to the three children for the first time. (Note that she did not give her name until the final apparition, so the children in the meantime referred to her as the Beautiful Lady.) Our Lady said, "I come from Heaven. I want you children to come here on the thirteenth of every month at the same hour (about noon). In the month of October I shall tell you who I am and what I want you to do."

Lucia asked if the three children would go to Heaven. The Lady replied, "Yes, you will all three go to Heaven, but Francisco will first have to say many Rosaries." She also said that she would take Francisco and Jacinta soon.

Lucia asked about two boy playmates. Our Lady responded, "One is in Heaven already, and the other is in Purgatory."

Then Lucia asked about a person she knew called Amelia. Our Lady said, "Amelia will be in Purgatory until the end of the world." *(Note that this prophecy was in question by many because it seemed so harsh. But many years later, when Lucia was questioned by a priest friend, she clarified the situation. Lucia said, "Amelia was 18 years old, Father, and, after all, for one mortal sin a soul may be in Hell forever.")*

After the apparition, the parish priest in Fatima remained skeptical about the possibility of the apparitions. Many others, including family members and relatives, thought that everything might be a trick from the devil. Also, the village authorities were extremely upset and did not believe anything supernatural was happening. As a result, the children had to suffer much from the ridicule and unbelief.

- June 13, 1917. Our Lady appeared to the children for the second time. About 60 people observed. (Of course, they could not see the vision.) During this apparition our Lady told the children to add the following prayer after each decade of the Rosary. "Oh, my Jesus, forgive us our sins. Save us from the fires of Hell and lead all souls to Heaven, especially those in most need of Thy Mercy."

- July 13, 1917. Our Lady appeared to the children for the third time. About 5,000 people observed. The children asked the Lady, "Why don't you work a miracle so that all the people will know that you really do appear to us?" Our Lady replied, "In October I will tell you who I am and will work a miracle so great that all will believe in the reality of the apparitions."

During this apparition the children were given three secrets which were not to be revealed until years later. The children were shown a vision of Hell. It was so terrible that Lucia later declared that the children would have died of fright were it not for the fact that the Blessed Lady was standing beside them and had already assured them that they would go to Heaven. The second secret was a prophecy that stated if people do not cease to offend God, another war (World War II) would break out and be even worse than the war in progress (World War I). It also projected the rise of Communist Russia who would spread her errors throughout the world. But she went on to say that, ***"In the end, my Immaculate Heart will triumph."*** The third secret had to do with a prophecy about a future Pope, and that he would have much to suffer. According to the message, there would be a figure clothed in white (a Pope traditionally wears a white cassock) who in battle appears to fall to the ground, presumably dead. *(Of note here is that Pope John Paul II was shot and wounded by an assassin on May 13, 1981, the anniversary of the first apparition at Fatima. According to the Pope, it was our Lady who guided the bullet to narrowly miss his vital organs. He later acknowledged that he was likely the Pope shown in the Fatima vision. The Popes actual words are as follows. "Could I forget that the event in St. Peter's Square took place on the day and at the hour when the first appearance of the Mother of Christ to the poor little peasants has been remembered for over sixty years at Fatima, Portugal? For in everything that happened to me on that very day, I felt that extraordinary motherly protection and care, which turned out to be stronger than the deadly bullet." In gratitude for the intervention of our Lady, the Pope gave one of the deadly bullets to the bishop in charge of the shrine at Fatima, Portugal. To this day, that bullet remains in the crown of the statue of the Blessed Virgin Mary housed at that shrine.)*

- August 19, 1917. Our Lady appeared to the children the fourth time. She was upset because the local public authorities had imprisoned the children for three days to prevent them from attending the apparition which was scheduled for August 13th. The authorities even threatened the children with death unless they recanted their story. Our Lady told the children that the planned miracle for October would be less striking as a result of the actions by the town administrators. During this apparition the Beautiful Lady told the children that many souls were lost forever because there was nobody to make sacrifices and to pray for them. As in every Fatima apparition, Mary emphasized that we should pray the Rosary every day.

- September 13, 1917. Our Lady appeared the fifth time. About 30,000 people were present. A luminous globe appeared in the sky and was visible to the attendees as it glided across the sky and to the place where the children were waiting. Suddenly a great shower of white roses fell from the heavens, reached almost to earth, and then dissolved from sight. During the conversation with the children, the Lady divulged for the first time some details of the great miracle to take place in October. She said that the Child Jesus and Saint Joseph would be with her and that some of the sick in the crowd would be healed.

- October 13, 1917. Our Lady appeared the sixth and final time. About 60,000 people were there in a driving and cold rainstorm. During the conversation with the children, the Beautiful Lady announced, *"I am the Lady of the Rosary."* She went on to say, *"People must amend their lives, ask pardon for their sins, and not offend Our Lord any more for He is already too greatly offended."* As predicted, the children also saw a vision of the Holy Family with Jesus, Mary, and Joseph.

- Then came what is known as the *Miracle of the Sun*. Gradually the sun grew pale, lost its normal color, and appeared as a silver disk which all could gaze at without shading their eyes. Then rays of color shot out as the sun spun like a wheel and danced in the sky. Then the sun appeared to break loose from its place in the heavens and hurled towards earth. The crowd screamed hysterically as they thought it was the end of the world. Suddenly the sun reversed course and returned to its accustomed place.

The trembling people looked at one another and were astonished. Their rain-sodden garments had suddenly dried and everybody felt comfortable and warm.

This Miracle of the Sun is considered to be one of the greatest miracles of our times.

Miracle of the Sun

As you may recall, our Lady of the Rosary predicted in the first apparition in 1917 that she would take Francisco and Jacinta to Heaven soon. Francisco died two years later, in 1919, and Jacinta died three years later, in 1920. Lucia became a cloistered nun and died in 2005 at the age of ninety-seven.

The Catholic Church strongly supports the Fatima messages as being of supernatural origin. As mentioned above, Saint Pope John Paul II believes that our Lady of Fatima protected him from the assassin's bullet when he was shot in Rome on the Feast of Our Lady of Fatima, May 13, 1981.

About four million pilgrims visit the Shine of Fatima every year. My wife and I were blessed with the opportunity to visit Fatima in September of 2012. Thank You, God! Thank you, Blessed Mother, Lady of the Rosary!

Our Lady of Mount Carmel at Garabandal

In 1961 in the village of Garabandal in Spain, four young girls ages eleven to twelve reported seeing Saint Michael the Archangel and then later, the Blessed Virgin Mary. These apparitions continued until 1965.

The apparitions in Garabandal have not yet been officially approved by the Catholic Church. But Saint Padre Pio confirmed to questioners that our Lady did indeed appear there. *(Note that Saint Padre Pio is one of the most revered Saints of recent times. He died in 1968 and was canonized as a saint in 2002. He is the first and only priest to receive the Stigmata, that is, the wounds of Christ.)*

There were countless appearances by our Lady, usually at random times. The four girls often experienced ecstasies. There were numerous phenomena reported. For example, the girls ran with great speed down steep mountainsides, even backwards, so that it was impossible for the astonished spectators to follow them. Their bodies did not seem to be subject to the law of gravity, but endowed with some sort of spiritual agility. There was also a miracle, forecast fifteen days in advance, whereby one of the visionaries received Holy Communion from an

Angel. The image of this Host appearing on her tongue was captured in a photograph.

The only other person to see Our Blessed Mother at Garabandal was a 38-year-old Spanish Jesuit Priest, Father Luis Marie Andreu. He was heard to say "Miracle! Miracle!" which is believed to be a vision of a future miracle proving that the apparitions at Garabandal and the associated messages should be believed. Father was so overcome that he died the same night. But his final words before he died were the following.

> "Oh! What a sweet and lovely Mother we have in Heaven… how happy I am… what a favor the Blessed Virgin has bestowed on me. How fortunate we are to have a Mother like her in Heaven! There is no reason to fear the supernatural life. The girls have given us an example of how we must act with the Blessed Virgin. There is no doubt, in my mind, that the things involving the girls are true. Why should the Blessed Virgin have chosen us? This is the happiest day of my life."

With those words, Father bowed his head and died. Our Lady has said, "…on the day after the future miracle, his body will be found to be incorrupt." *(Note: the future miracle has not happened yet.)*

The visionaries reported receiving two messages: the first directly from the Blessed Virgin Mary; and the second from the Virgin Mary by way of Saint Michael the Archangel. The messages are as follows.

> October 18, 1961. (From Our Mother.) We must make many sacrifices, perform much penance, and visit the Blessed Sacrament frequently. But first, we must lead good lives. If we do not, a chastisement will befall us. The cup is already filling up and, if we do not change, a very great chastisement will come upon us.

June 18th 1965. (Four years later. Since the content of this message pained Our Lady so much it was given instead by St Michael the Archangel.) As my message of October 18th has not been complied with and has not been made known to the world, I am advising you that this is the last one. Before, the cup was filling up. Now it is flowing over. Many cardinals, many bishops, and many priests are on the road to perdition and are taking many souls with them. Less and less importance is being given to the Eucharist. You should turn the wrath of God away from yourselves by your efforts. If you ask His forgiveness with sincere hearts, He will pardon you. I, your mother, through the intercession of Saint Michael the Archangel, ask you to amend your lives. You are now receiving the last warnings. I love you very much and do not want your condemnation. Pray to us with sincerity and we will grant your requests. You should make more sacrifices. Think about the passion of Jesus.

There were four predictions given by Our Mother at Garabandal about the future.

1. Following a time of *tribulation* there will be a *worldwide warning* in which everyone will see the state of their soul before God. We will see the damage caused by our sins and the good we have omitted doing. The warning will come when the tribulation will be at its worst and when the warning will be most needed.

2. Within a year after the warning a *miracle* will take place in Garabandal. It will be announced eight days beforehand by one of the girls who knows the date.

It can be seen and televised and all the sick who will be present will be healed.

3. A *permanent visible sign* will be left at Garabandal, a sign for unbelievers. In at least one other apparition Our Lady has promised the same.

4. If we still do not convert a *chastisement* will befall the world. This was also predicted by Our Lady at Akita in Japan in an apparition approved by the Church.

Keep in mind that the Church has not yet approved the apparitions at Garabandal, and has also not approved or agreed with the predictions. But neither have they condemned them as untrue. In any case, Garabandal has proven to be of considerable interest to the faithful. And generally speaking, the messages are consistent with the Bible and with other Marian messages: pray, sacrifice, and repent.

Mary and I were blessed to visit the village of Garabandal in September of 2012.

Our Lady of Kibeho in Rwanda

These apparitions are not nearly as well known as many of the others, but in some ways are very dramatic. Also, they are recent history having occurred only thirty-five years ago.

These apparitions began in November of 1981 to three teenage African girls who were attending high school in the town of Kibeho, Rwanda. The vision given by the Blessed Virgin Mary on August 19, 1982 was apocalyptic. *She asked everyone to pray to prevent a terrible war.* As part of the vision, the children saw dismembered corpses and rivers flowing red with blood.

Twelve years later, in 1994, this vision came to fruition. As a result of an internal Civil War between two ethnic factions, approximately one million Rwandans were killed. Most of them were hacked to death by machetes wielded by their neighbors. The rivers were literally red with blood. All of this happened over a three month period. The genocide is well documented by one of the survivors whose name is **Immaculee Ilibagiza**. Her initial book describing this is called **Left To Tell**. During that terrible three months she stayed in a small hidden bathroom with seven other women in a pastor's home. Her weight dropped from 115 to 65 pounds.

Immaculee survived and lived to tell the story. To experience her own healing, she explained how it was necessary for her to forgive the killers of her family. These killers were neighbors who had been helped by her family prior to the genocide. Today Immaculee is regarded as one of world's leading speakers on peace, faith, and forgiveness.

The apparitions by the three teenage girls have been approved by the Catholic Church. A sanctuary was built at the site of the high school and is named "Shrine of Our Lady of Sorrows."

I have not had the opportunity to visit this site.

Our Lady Queen of Peace at Medjugorje

The visions at Medjugorje are the most comprehensive in the history of the world. *They have been occurring daily for the last 35 years!*

On June 24, 1981, on the feast day of Saint John the Baptist, the Blessed Virgin Mary appeared for the first time to six children who ranged in age from ten to seventeen. The visions happened in what was then called the country of Croatia, located across the Adriatic Sea from Italy.

Why is Our Lady appearing? Here is what she has said about that:

> *"I have come to call the world to <u>conversion</u> (of heart) for the last time. Afterwards I will not appear any more on this earth."*

The Blessed Virgin Mary explains that *conversion of heart* comes about by focusing on four basic activities:

> *prayer, peace, fasting, and penance.*

The names of the six visionaries are as follows: Marija, Marjana, Ivanka, Ivan, Vicka, and Jakov.

One intriguing aspect related to these six visionaries is the meaning of their names in the Croatian language:

- The names Marija and Mirjana both mean "Mary," which is the Blessed Mother's name.
- The names Ivanka and Ivan mean "John." *Our Lady first appeared on June 24, 1981, which is the Feast of Saint John the Baptist. His message was one of repentance and a declaration that the Kingdom of Heaven was at hand. John the Baptist prepared the way for the first coming of the Messiah.*
- The name Vicka means "life." Our Lady has revealed to Vicka her life story, which Vicka is to make public when Our Lady tells her to do so.
- Finally, the name Jakov means "James." The only parish church in Medjugorje is named Saint James.

Clearly the names of the visionary children are no coincidence, but rather something ordained by our providential God. (Remember: There are no accidents!) Incredible!

Our Lady still appears on a *daily* basis to three of the visionaries: Ivan, Marija, and Vicka. Marija receives *one message a month* that is intended for distribution to the whole world. The other three visionaries, Mirjana, Ivanka, and Jakov no longer see Our Lady daily. Our Lady has promised that she will appear to them *once a year* for the rest of their lives.

These six visionaries were tested by scientists to validate the authenticity of the visions. During these visions they were connected to electronic equipment and poked with needles. Their brain waves were measured. The testing confirmed that an extraordinary experience was taking place, and that the results were simultaneous among the six children.

My wife, Mary, and I had the opportunity to personally visit

Medjugorje in November of 2003. But the big experience we had as a family came as a result of a visit by our daughter, Angela, in August of 1991. At that time Angela was about to begin her third year of college and was searching for the truth. Upon learning that these apparitions were occurring, she paid her own way and went with a group to a scheduled youth conference there. While there she experienced more than one miracle. But the most significant miracle happened while she was attending Eucharistic adoration. At that time, while praying in front of the consecrated host (i.e. the body and blood of our Lord Jesus Christ) she heard Jesus speak to her. He said,

"It is I, Who am here. It is I, Who stands before you! It is I, Who shall grant you your heart's desire."

Needless to say, this resulted in an instantaneous change in Angela's perception of life. Upon returning from Medjugorje, she dramatically changed her way of living. She ultimately found a like-minded Catholic named Tim, married him, and the rest is history.

But it didn't stop there. Angela's explosion of faith then infected the rest of our family. In the end, it changed each and every one of us. Since then each family member has had their own miracles, but Medjugorje was the event, and Angela was the person, that affected everything which followed. Over the years several of our children and their spouses have had the opportunity to make a pilgrimage to Medjugorje. They too have had life-changing experiences. Praise God!

Now I have to add a special note here. Although the visible experience of our family's conversion of heart was as a result of Angela's exciting conversion, it needs to be said that for the twenty-five years preceding this event, my wife, Mary, prayed for something like this to happen. She prayed that her family would become more holy. Who says prayer doesn't work? Wow! Thank You, God! Thank you, Blessed Virgin Mary! And thank you, my dear wife, for your persistence. You knocked and you knocked and the door was opened!

O O O

If you want to find out more about Medjugorje, and I recommend you do, then a good place to start is the website www.medjugorje.com. Also you might want to read the first book I read about Medjugorje which is called *Queen of the Cosmos* by Jan Connell. It contains interviews with the child visionaries which were collected shortly after the visions began. This book is very easy to read and the children's responses are beautiful in their simplicity and innocence. Ms. Connell has also written a follow-on book which is more thorough. It is called *The Visions of the Children*.

The Medjugorje website has an incredible collection of information, including all the messages given by Our Lady, descriptions of Heaven, Hell, and Purgatory based on what was shown to some of the visionaries, information about some of the miracles that have occurred, and much more.

One of the miracles that may not be documented on the website is the story about Marija and a young Italian man who was interested in dating her. The problem was that he spoke only Italian and she spoke only Croatian. So Our Lady gave Marija a gift. Her gift was the ability to instantly speak fluent Italian! The result? They are now married and have four sons. Is that cool or what!

Recently I had the opportunity to hear the testimony of Arthur (Artie) Boyle. I briefly mentioned his healing earlier this book. To recap, Artie was told by his doctors that he had inoperable cancer and only six months to live. He became so depressed with the news that he could barely walk. Meanwhile, his faithful wife, his family, and his friends prayed incessantly for his healing. Eventually someone suggested that he fly to Medjugorje where the Virgin Mary was appearing and where others had received miraculous healings.

Artie flew over to Medjugorje with two of his good friends and, after his arrival, engaged in all the pilgrimage activities. One of the primary activities in Medjugorje is *Sacramental Confession*. Artie, a Catholic from birth, had not been to confession for fifteen years. He went and cleansed his soul of all his sins. Then he was also led to *forgive* certain people in his life. *Through these actions he was healed spiritually.*

Then the Spirit led him through prayer and circumstances to receive his ***physical healing***. Upon returning to the Boston area, his doctors were shocked and mystified about the changes they saw. They confirmed that there is no medical explanation for Artie to be alive today.

Artie has an explanation, however. He knows that God wanted him healed spiritually, and that was the priority of God. It was also in God's plan for him to be healed physically. Artie firmly believes that he was healed by Jesus Christ through the intercession of the Blessed Virgin Mary *(who is still appearing daily to some of the Visionaries)*.

Artie has captured his testimony in a book entitled, ***Six Months to Live: Three Guys on the Ultimate Quest for a Miracle***. It makes for great reading.

On a personal note, as Artie was giving his testimony, there were a few times I had all I could do to not burst out sobbing. Why? It is because when I see God's mercy in action, it touches me deeply.

Now back to the Medjugorje website and the information there. One of the stories that intrigued me was about the physical healing of a person who was a member of a different religion. A Roman Catholic Priest was confused. The Blessed Virgin Mary provided some insight into this healing by giving the following response to a visionary *(her response demonstrates that God does not belong to one religion!)*.

Our Lady said, "Tell this priest, tell everyone, that it is you who are divided on earth. The ***Muslims*** and the ***Orthodox***, for the same reason as ***Catholics***, are equal before my Son and me. You are all my children. ***Certainly, all religions are not equal, but all men are equal before God, as Saint Paul says.*** It does not suffice to belong to the Catholic Church to be saved, but it is necessary to respect the commandments of God in following one's conscience. Those who are not Catholics are no less creatures made in the image of God and are destined to someday rejoin the House of the Father. ***Salvation is available to everyone, without exception. Only those who refuse God deliberately are condemned.*** To him who has been given little,

little will be asked for. To whomever has been given much, very much will be required. *It is God alone, in His infinite justice, Who determines the degree of responsibility and pronounces judgment.*"

Marian Apparitions - Conclusion

So what is the meaning of all these apparitions? Why are they significant?

To me, essentially, *they give us all hope!* While we can talk about God and theorize and speculate and wonder and conclude, how much of what we believe is concrete versus how much is our own imagination? The advantage of these apparitions whereby the Blessed Virgin Mary is sent to us as a messenger from God is that we have something concrete and specific to believe and to focus on. Her messages are not new. Her messages are right out of the Bible. The message is, in fact, in the messenger herself. While the words provide no new information over and above the Bible and the teachings of the Catholic Church, they serve to emphasize aspects that require more focus. We need to eliminate a lot of our distractions and take specific actions.

It is also significant that God the Father chose the Blessed Virgin Mary to deliver these messages. They could be delivered by an Angel, or by Jesus himself, or by the Holy Spirit. It appears, however, that from a mass marketing standpoint, the Blessed Virgin Mary was chosen to lead the worldwide effort to convert hearts.

I also believe that because the first appearance at Medjugorje by our Blessed Mother was on the Feast of Saint John the Baptist, that this is a significant message in and of itself. John the Baptist came to announce the First Coming of Jesus. I believe that in this era the Blessed Mother is the current day John the Baptist, announcing the Second Coming of Jesus. Now we all know Jesus will be coming to us personally the day we die, which for some of us could be tomorrow. But taking the whole world into consideration, I am definitely convinced that she is also trying to give the entire world a message that we are about to experience the Second Coming. Now the manner of this Second Coming may not be perfectly defined or understood. It might already be happening in some way. But I will personally guarantee that something is going on that is extremely significant from a spiritual standpoint.

So what should we do differently?

It is very simple. ***We need to increase the sense of <u>urgency</u> with which we live our lives.*** We need to convert our hearts! We need to focus on our objective which is to live our life the way Jesus tells us in the Bible. Furthermore, we need to follow His directive which is described in the Gospel of Matthew, Chapter 28:16-20: we must go out and proclaim to the world the Good News:

Christ has died! Christ is risen! Christ will come again!

And, according to Saint Francis of Assisi, we must go out in the world and ***live the Gospel and, if necessary, use words***. We need to bring others with us when we leave this life and enter the next life.

And the Blessed Virgin Mary, our Mother, our loving Mother, our spiritual Mother, will lead us to Jesus who will then lead us to the Father where we will bask in the glory of His Presence for Eternity.

Amen.

Urgent Advice: A Recap

The following is a summary of the ***urgent advice*** I am passing on to you, my grandchildren, and to everyone who needs a grandpa!

- There is a God. There are three persons in the one God: Father, Son, and Holy Spirit. You are not God.
- You are in a relationship with each person of God: you have a Father, a Brother, and a Spouse. You must nurture this relationship with ***constant prayer***.
- You have a spiritual Mother: Mary of Nazareth. Her role is to lead us to the Father through Jesus in the Holy Spirit. She is the Ark of the Covenant.
- Since God is your Father, you are a member of a powerful royal family! You are a prince! You are a princess!
- You have a mission. Your mission is to get into the Ark and convince others to get into the Ark with you. ***There are NO ACCIDENTS;*** there are NO COINCIDENCES! Everything that happens to you is a gift from God to support your mission.
- You must make decisions which conform to your mission:
  - ***Decide and commit to obey God 100%***
  - Decide to live a clean and pure life
  - Decide to allow God to choose your college, your spouse, and your job
  - Decide to be a servant to others.
  - Decide to be happy: radiate joy

- o Decide to be compassionate: cry with others
- o ***Decide to allow God to help you choose how you spend the gift of your time on a moment-by-moment basis***
- o ***Decide to forgive others (and yourself) seventy-seven times***
- You must be constantly aware that your extremely competent Enemy never sleeps. Satan will do everything to undermine your mission. To protect yourself, jump into the arms of your spiritual Mother, Mary. It is she who will crush his head with her heel!
- Jesus gave us the Pope and the Catholic Church to be His visible presence on Earth. Embrace that divine gift with gratitude and humility.

Just remember, I love you! Your grandma loves you. Your entire family loves you. We are all striving for Heaven where we can spend Eternity together. We want you to join us. Heaven is where <u>you</u> will find family. <u>Decide</u>!

Love,
Grandpa Young

Appendices: The Basics of Catholicism

Appendix I. The Big Picture

The **decision making framework** for a faithful Catholic is based on the **Bible**, and summarized in the **Creed**, which is shown in Appendix V. *Basically, we believe there is one God with three persons: Father, Son, and Holy Spirit. God is the creator of everything; He is also the sustainer of everything. He keeps the entire Universe in existence. God the <u>Father</u> sent His only Son, <u>Jesus</u> (the God-man) to the earth 2000 years ago to reveal Himself to us so that we have the proper understanding of how we should live our lives in order to join God in Heaven when we die and pass into the next phase of our life.* We also know from the **Bible** that the earthly human mother of Jesus is named **Mary of Nazareth**. She is in Heaven now with her Son, Jesus, along with all the other Saints. We also believe that when Jesus left the earth and ascended into Heaven, He sent the **Holy Spirit**, the third person of the **Holy Trinity**, to be with us on earth until the end of the world.

In addition to the Bible and the Creed, we have as part of our decision making framework the **Catholic Catechism**, which has been developed by the teaching authority of the Church (that is, **the Pope and Bishops — the <u>Magisterium</u>**). The purpose of the Catholic Catechism is to interpret the teachings of Jesus in the context of our modern society. This relationship of the Magisterium, the Bible, Tradition, and the Catholic Catechism is shown in the following Figure A.

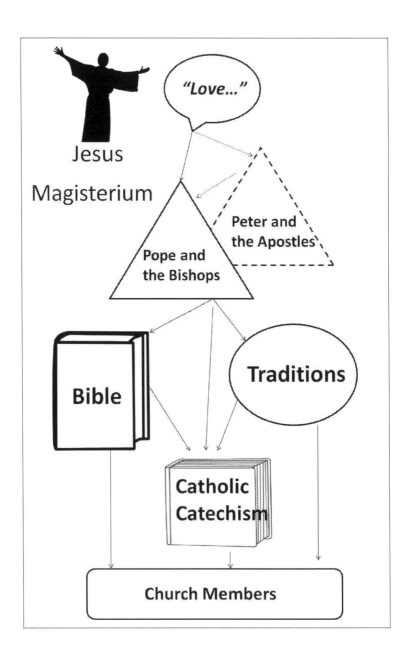

Appendix II. God Exists!

In this book, *the word "God" refers to a supreme being with infinite knowledge and unlimited power Who is perfectly good and all loving and Who is present everywhere. Furthermore, He created the Universe and keeps the Universe in existence.* Whew! Got it?

So, does this supreme being, called GOD, exist? Or is He just a figment of our human imagination?

I believe that God exists. But how can I convince you?

How does a fish convince his fellow fish that water exists? How does a bird convince fellow birds that air exists? How does a dog convince other dogs that humans have more intelligence than dogs?

It is beyond the scope of this book to prove to you that God exists. Brilliant philosophers and scientists have for centuries discussed and debated the question about the existence of God. When I was taking a philosophy course in college, the class was taught about the five proofs of God developed by Saint Thomas Aquinas. If you want to dig into the discussion of the existence of God, merely go to the internet, Wikipedia, and browse the topic "Existence of God." Interesting. Included there is a brief synopsis of the five proofs by Saint Thomas Aquinas and also a summary of the teaching by the Catholic Church. Also covered under this topic in Wikipedia is a summary of what Atheists believe about the non-existence of God. The Aquinas argument that I find most valuable is the explanation that, in our Universe, every effect has a cause. Everything that happens is caused by a preceding event. Using this logic, there has to be a primal cause, which we call "God."

As your loving grandpa, I will tell you from my <u>experience</u> that God does, in fact, exist.

If someone does want to understand some basic reasoning, refer them to the *"Intelligent Design" Theory*. This theory essentially states that the ordered universe could NOT happen without a Divine Designer. The existence of human beings with the ability to make moral choices guided by a conscience could NOT exist without a Divine Designer. It is illogical and foolish to conclude otherwise.

And you should not be intimidated by a pseudo-intellectual who wants to argue about the existence of God. They might even have the initials "Ph.D." behind their name, but in some circles that means "piled higher and deeper."

So, if you happen to come across someone who tells you that there is no God, and that the Universe was created by a spontaneous Big Bang, just smile knowingly and say to them, "Yeah... right...." Pause a moment, and then continue, "In my family we give the Big Bang another name. We call Him GOD!"

Now for the *sincere questioner* who really wants to know if there is a God, I suggest they do what my daughter, Heather, did. She wanted to believe, but felt like she was going through the motions and did not really know why she should continue practicing her faith. So she prayed, "God, if You really do exist, then show me. And show me why You are relevant in my life." She asked it sincerely and was open to the response. God answered her in a dramatic way. You can find out more by listening to her testimony at my website **www.calltobefree.com**.

The critical question addressed in this book is not about the existence of God, but about the follow-on question: *So what?*

Appendix III.
History According to Grandpa

History of the World

The world happened like this. The world was created by God. Then God created one man and one woman. They had some kids. Those kids had some kids. Those kids had some kids. At the current time, we have a little over seven billion kids on this planet earth (that is 7,000,000,000).

Since the beginning of this planet there were times of peace and times of war. During the times of peace, everyone prospered and was happy. During times of war, a lot of people got killed and people were upset.

A lot of people were born. With the exception of the 7 billion people living today, every single one of them died.

Some people lived a very short time. And some lived a long time. One hundred years is considered a long time for the life of a person.

For all practical purposes, that pretty much covers the relevant history of the world.

History of Religion

The history of religion can be quite interesting. The good news is this: the Jewish culture was extremely accomplished at keeping records. They started keeping records in approximately 2000 BC (2000 years before Jesus Christ was born). It was about that time that the concept of

monotheism came into human consciousness. The word mono-theism means "one God." Prior to that time, people believed in *polytheism.* Polytheism is when people believe in more than one God. For example they believe that the sun is god, the moon is god, a specific rock is god, and so forth. And so the concept of monotheism by the Jewish people was unique at the time. Furthermore, what was even more unique, was that this God was an unseen God. He was a *spiritual being* who was not visible to the human eye. The Jewish people referred to their God by the name of Yahweh.

We will talk about the Bible later, but essentially the Old Testament section of the Bible is the history of monotheism from the year 2000 BC to the year 1 AD.

Which requires me to deviate from the topic somewhat. What happened in the year 1 AD? The net of it is this. There was a God-man, whose name is ***Jesus Christ***, who was born at that time. He had such an impact on human history that all historical time was put in the framework of His arrival on earth. Thus B.C. stands for Before Christ; and A.D. stands for Anno Domini, which is Latin for "In the year of our Lord."

The next period of time, or era, is from the year 1 AD to the year 33 AD. This is the span of time during which the God-man, named Jesus, lived on earth.

Then there's the era from 33 AD to 313 AD. During this timeframe the followers of this God-man, who were called Christians, began to practice their religion in very difficult circumstances. Initially most of the Christians were converts from the Jewish faith (Judaism). In fact, Jesus Christ was Jewish. His mother was Jewish, His father was Jewish, His grandparents were Jewish. During this period of time the Jewish people referred to those outside their faith and culture as *gentiles.* Eventually some of these gentiles became Christians also. The most notable convert from Judaism to Christianity was Paul of Tarsus. We refer to him as Saint Paul.

This group of Christians became outcasts to both the Jews and the gentiles. They were persecuted and frequently killed.

Despite this, however, the number of Christians grew rapidly. It seemed like the more you killed them, the more they multiplied. Interesting phenomenon.

Just a little more background. During this era the Romans (from Rome) were essentially rulers of the world — that is, the world as known today by what is called Europe and the Middle East.

In the year 313 AD, the emperor of Rome, whose name was Constantine, changed everything through an executive order. Emperors, and sometimes United States presidents, have the power to do this (that is, executive orders). In this case, Constantine is believed to be heavily influenced by his mother, Saint Helena, who became convinced that Jesus Christ was, in fact, a God-man and that the Christian faith was the true faith. So the Emperor Constantine decreed that Christianity was instantly legal in the entire Roman Empire. And as a result, many people in the Roman Empire became Christian over the next several centuries.

Now in the year 622 AD along came a man named **Mohammed**. Mohammed did not claim to be God, but he did claim to be a prophet. And from his point of view, Jesus was not a God-man but rather a man who was also a prophet. A prophet is a human who speaks for God. The Jewish faith had many prophets as is documented in the Old Testament of the Bible. Some of the more familiar Jewish prophets are Isaiah, Jeremiah, and Ezekiel.

Mohammed wrote a book called the **Koran**. The people who use this book, the Koran, as the basis for their faith and their understanding of God became known as **Muslims**. Their faith is called **Islam**. It is a monotheistic religion, as is Judaism and Christianity. They believe in one God. They refer to their God as **Allah**.

So from the year 622 AD until the present time, there remain three major monotheistic religions: Judaism, Christianity, and Islam. They all believe in one God. This God has a different name in each religion. And this God is a spirit.

<u>Christianity is unique</u> in that it believes that this one God consists of three persons and one of the persons (Jesus Christ) was

incarnated (covered with flesh; became human). The other persons in the one God of Christianity are God the Father and God the Holy Spirit.

Eventually an organization was created to solidify the practice and teachings of the Christians. This organization was called the Catholic Church. The word *catholic* means *universal*. And in the time of Rome, the Catholic Church was, in fact, universal within the realm of the Roman Empire.

The overall timing of monotheism is shown in the following Figure B.

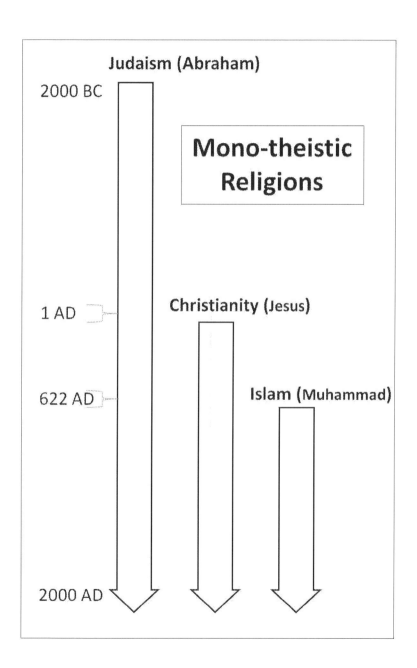

History of the Bible

Okay let's talk briefly about the Bible.

All Christians believe that the Bible is the inspired word of God. The heart of the Bible is considered to be the four Gospels: Matthew, Mark, Luke, and John. These four Gospels (also called "books") of the Bible record what Jesus said and did during His three years of public ministry from the years 30 to 33 AD.

The Bible consists of two major sections: the Old Testament and the New Testament. The Old Testament is essentially a 2000+ year history of the Jewish faith. The New Testament begins with the birth of Jesus and records the events from His birth until about seventy years later.

Now how did the Bible come about?

The Old Testament was developed by the Jewish scholars who collected and maintained this information over the centuries. Much of it was passed down verbally. It was a lot like your grandpa's stories. They would sit around the campfire and tell them over and over. It is possible the stories got a little exaggerated along the way. But while the historical accuracy may be in question, *the Catholic Church contends that these stories (called books) are divinely inspired by God and are true in terms of faith and moral teachings.* Did God really create the world in seven days as described in the Bible? Well it could have been six days or eight days. Or a day could mean a million years. *The message is that God did create the world. And furthermore, He created human beings.* The details are not particularly important. No knowledgeable Christian expects the Bible to be scientifically accurate.

Similarly, the New Testament consists of stories and teachings related to the life and teachings of Jesus that were initially told verbally. Later on as the Apostles and other disciples of Jesus realized that His promised Second Coming was not imminent, they started to write things down to document them.

These *sacred writings* of both the Old and New Testaments were only a part of all the writings that were available in the early years of Christianity.

(Note: The term "catholic" was used in the year 107 AD in reference to Christians. The word "catholic" means "universal." This usage of the word "catholic" continued to become more prevalent. Finally, in the year 380 AD, the term "Catholic" Christianity was used by the Roman Empire when they declared "Catholic" Christianity as the official state religion.)

In the year 393 AD, the Catholic Church decided which of the historical writings were to be considered "sacred" and therefore included in what is now called the Bible. **Note that some of the early writings were included and some were not.** One key criteria for inclusion was the decision by the Pope and other Catholic bishops about whether or not a particular writing was **divinely inspired, or sacred.** *(Of note is that the Pope and other Catholic Bishops are the "teaching authority" of the Catholic Church and are referred to as the **Magisterium**.)*

The content of the Bible has remained relatively unchanged from 393 AD to the present day, with one exception. In the year 1517 AD, a Catholic priest in Germany by the name of Martin Luther rebelled against the authority of the church. He and his followers ultimately created a new version of the Bible which is a subset of the Catholic version. The rebellious movement became known as the **Protestant Reformation**, and spawned the Lutheran Church, the Methodist Church, and literally thousands of other churches that are Christian in belief but not organizationally connected to the Catholic-Christian Church.

The original Protestant (i.e. non-Catholic Christian) subset of the Catholic version of the Bible excludes a handful of books in the Old Testament. The logic for this was that, in general, the Old Testament was written in Hebrew and the New Testament was written in Greek. Since a Hebrew version of some Old Testament books could not be found at the time of Martin Luther, the Protestants chose to exclude them from their version of the Bible. Subsequently, it has been determined that some of these excluded books from the Protestant Bible were, in fact, written in Hebrew. They discovered this when they recently (1946 AD) found the Dead Sea Scrolls. Since then these excluded books may be included in some way in the Protestant Bibles. The list of excluded books includes, for example, Tobit, Sirach, and Baruch.

The other historically relevant factor is the language translations that occur. For example, the Hebrew and Greek words need to be translated into English for Americans to understand the content. In this regard, the Catholics and non-Catholic Christians have cooperated and have generally agreed on the most recent English translation called the NRSV, or New Revised Standard Version, of the Bible.

The overall timing of the Bible construction is shown in the following Figure C.

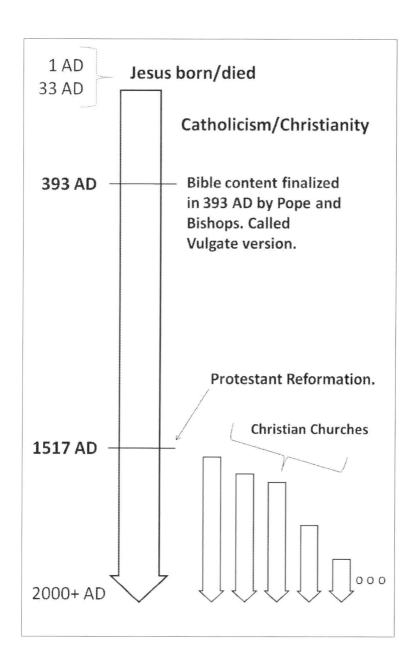

1 AD
33 AD
— Jesus born/died

Catholicism/Christianity

393 AD — Bible content finalized in 393 AD by Pope and Bishops. Called Vulgate version.

Protestant Reformation.

Christian Churches

1517 AD

2000+ AD

o o o

What are some key aspects of the Bible?

The primary message in the Old Testament is that God has a special relationship with the Jewish people. They have an agreement which is called a **covenant**. That basic agreement is as follows: I will be your God and you will be My people. That is why the Jewish people often refer to themselves as "the chosen people."

One of the critical texts in the Old Testament is established when the most important prophet in Judaism, Moses, has an encounter with God and receives the **Ten Commandments**. The Ten Commandments are considered to be the essence of the moral code of both Judaism and Christianity. *The first three commandments essentially say "Love God"; the last seven essentially say "Love your neighbor."* The Ten Commandments are listed in Appendix VI.

Several books of the Old Testament contain the writings of the "prophets." Of these prophets, probably the most well-known is the prophet Isaiah. It is in his book that the prophet Isaiah foretells the coming of the **Messiah**. The Jewish people believed that this Messiah was going to free them from their slavery to their oppressors, which at the time of Jesus were the Romans. They believed that this Messiah was going to be a strong military and political leader. The Jewish people who did not recognize Jesus Christ as the Messiah did not become Christians.

The first three books of the New Testament are called the **Synoptic Gospels** and are named for their authors **Matthew, Mark, and Luke**. They record the three years of the public ministry of Jesus. *The fourth Gospel is the Book of John*, which was written by the Apostle John. John's book has the history similar to the three synoptic Gospels, but goes far beyond that and includes many mystical theological concepts that John acquired as a result of his special relationship with both Jesus and His mother, Mary, both before and after the crucifixion.

According to the Gospels, Peter, one of the original twelve Apostles, was named by Jesus to be the first __Pope__ — that is, the head of the Catholic/Christian church (Matthew 16:18-19).

The fifth book in the New Testament is called the **Acts of the**

Apostles. This book focuses on what happened immediately after the death of Jesus. It recounts how the Apostles spread the Gospel, that is the "good news," after Jesus was crucified.

Following this portion of the Bible are the ***letters from Saint Paul*** to several groups of people. Perhaps the most well-known and thorough letter is his letter to the Romans. Paul, whose original name was Saul, was not one of the original 12 Apostles. He became a convert to Christianity after the church started to grow following the death of Jesus. Saul started out persecuting the Christians. He was a well-educated Jew who was also a Roman citizen. He led the effort to have the new Christians arrested and thrown in jail. There they were often beaten. In fact, the Bible states that Saul (Paul) was present and approved when one of the first martyrs, Stephen, was stoned to death because he was a Christian (Acts 7:54-60).

But God had another plan for Saul. One day, while traveling to Damascus, he was knocked to the ground by the power of God (Acts 9:1-18). He heard a voice which said, "Why are you persecuting Me?" It was the voice of Jesus. Jesus was equating Himself to the church; thus by persecuting the Church, Saul was persecuting Jesus. Saul was blinded during this experience. He was instructed to go to Damascus and wait for orders. Eventually Jesus sent a man named Ananias to instruct Saul in the Christian faith. As a result of this conversion experience, Saul was renamed Paul and became an outspoken advocate for Christianity.

What is unique about the Catholic perspective of the Bible?

As mentioned previously, the Pope and Bishops are the teaching authority of the Catholic Church and determined the content of the Bible. All Christians, including Catholic-Christians, use the Bible as the primary basis for their belief. What can be different, however, is that the Catholic Church has the one teaching authority, referred to as the Magisterium. The Magisterium is responsible for ensuring that our interpretation is consistent within the entire Church and for translating the messages of faith and morals into words and concepts that our contemporary society can comprehend. For example, the Bible does not discuss artificial contraception which occurs as a result of using the birth control pill. That is because the underlying science of the pill did not exist at the time the Bible was written. Therefore the authority of the Catholic Church determines the morality of using this pill in the context of the overall message of the Bible.

The interpretation of the Bible, as well as the explanation of other key teachings of the Catholic Church, are contained in the book called the <u>Catechism of the Catholic Church</u>. The latest version of the Catechism was published in 1992 AD under the direction of Saint Pope John Paul II.

The Bible, along with the Catholic Catechism and other Sacred Traditions, are collectively referred to as the <u>Deposit of Faith</u>. The Magisterium has the responsibility to safeguard this precious gift from God.

For non-Catholic Christians, who have no central authority, this ability to translate the Biblical teachings into contemporary morality can be very problematic. That is why many Bible Christians have different beliefs about key aspects of the faith. Whereas for all practical purposes they implicitly accept the authority of the Catholic Church in determining which sacred writings constitute the Bible, they explicitly reject the concept of that authority today as a result of the rupture of the Church starting with Martin Luther.

The overall timing of Protestant Sects is shown in the following Figure D.

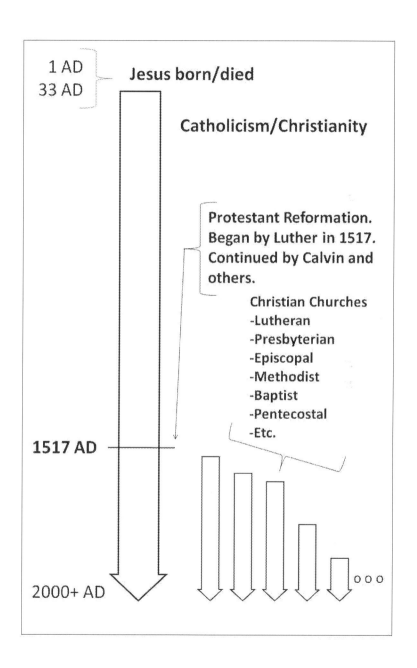

1 AD
33 AD

Jesus born/died

Catholicism/Christianity

Protestant Reformation.
Began by Luther in 1517.
Continued by Calvin and
others.

Christian Churches
-Lutheran
-Presbyterian
-Episcopal
-Methodist
-Baptist
-Pentecostal
-Etc.

1517 AD

2000+ AD

o o o

Should you read the Bible?

Of course you should read the Bible! My only advice, however, is to proceed with caution. If you suddenly want to read the entire Bible and start on page one, I suspect that by the time you get to page 300 you are going to be overwhelmed and give up. I have read the Bible from cover to cover. But you need a lot of time and need to be highly motivated. And before I decided to read it from cover to cover, I started by reading the four Gospels and the Acts of the Apostles. Then I read the book of Genesis and the letter of Saint Paul to the Romans and eventually I read Chapter 12 of the Book of Revelation. As I continued on my spiritual journey, I was led by the Spirit to read the Book of Job. This book is very helpful when you want to understand why bad things happen to good people.

Catholics tend to not read the Bible nearly as much as active non-Catholic Christians. It turns out that the way our public prayer is designed, that is, the Mass, the entire Bible is essentially covered over a period of three years. In other words, every Sunday key portions of both the Old and New Testaments are read. In addition, the priest gives a homily (sermon) on these readings.

If you are going to buy a Bible, and you should, it is important that Catholics purchase a Catholic version of the Bible. To start with, you should buy the Bible either from a Catholic bookstore or from an online Catholic source. Many Christian (non-Catholic) bookstores will not have a Catholic version of the Bible. The reason for selecting a Catholic Bible is so that you get a bible which includes the books which may be missing from the Protestant Bible. You also want to get a Bible which has all the cross-references at the bottom of each page. This is important because many of the writings in the New Testament refer back to writings in the Old Testament. These references are extremely helpful because when Jesus says something, He is often using the Old Testament writings to create a framework for His messages to the listeners of His time. I personally own the Saint Joseph edition of the New American Bible (the large type and illustrated addition) published by the Catholic Book Publishing Company.

Finally, as you begin to seriously consider reading the Bible, I would suggest that you watch the six hour movie called **Jesus of Nazareth**. It was produced in 1977. It will give you an overview of the Biblical story and help dramatize the action. There are several movies about Jesus floating around. Be careful. Many of them may be fictionally enhanced for purposes of entertainment and thus are less than accurate and can leave you confused.

Appendix IV. Is God Catholic?

Is God Catholic? Is God Christian? Is God Jewish? Is God Muslim? Using simple human logic, the answer to these questions can only be a resounding YES! How can that be?

If you look at each of the three monotheistic religions, they essentially all define God the same: spirit, one, all-powerful, creator of the world, sustainer of the world, and so forth. Thus, by definition, we are all praying to the same God! What is different, however, is how we perceive the one God. Let us review.

When we say we are Catholic, what does that mean? First of all that means we are Christian. And as we talked about earlier, to be Christian means to believe that Jesus Christ is the God-man. Furthermore we believe that there is one God, so we are monotheistic (mono means one; theism means God). As we mentioned in an earlier chapter, there are three religions that are monotheistic. They are Judaism, Christianity, and Islam. All three believe that there is one, unseen God who is the creator of the universe and the maintainer of the universe. Each religion has a name for this God. In Judaism God is called Yahweh. In Islam they use the name Allah to identify God. In Christianity there are three persons in the one God. The term "God" usually refers to God the Father who is one of the three persons. But it can also mean the three persons (i.e. the Blessed Trinity) in one God.

In relating to God, Christians spend a great deal of time and focus on the second person of this Blessed Trinity, Jesus Christ. The reason for this is that Christians believe that God the Father revealed Himself through His Son, Jesus Christ, who is mysteriously both fully God and fully man, and who continues to interact with His people on earth through the third person of the Holy Trinity whose name is the Holy Spirit.

As you recall in terms of historical sequence, Judaism came first and this is well documented in the Old Testament section of the Bible. This section represents about two-thirds of the words that are written in the Bible. It is essentially a history of the Jewish people over 2000 years of time. And it puts this history in the context of their relationship with this one, unseen God. Their relationship is described as a covenant or a contract with God whereby God said, "You are My people and I am your God."

Then in the year 1 AD a person by the name of Jesus was born to a woman called Mary of Nazareth. He was born in a town called Bethlehem in Israel. *(An interesting side note is that the word Bethlehem in Hebrew means "house of bread." Later Jesus describes himself as the "bread of life".)*

A fairly detailed description of what happened during the time Jesus was born, lived, and died is included in the New Testament of the Bible. ***The reason Christians think that Jesus is "God" is that He said He was. And He proved it by performing numerous miracles that included healing sick people and raising people from the dead.*** The reason the Jews had Jesus crucified by the Romans is because Jesus portrayed Himself as equal to Yahweh and thus committed "blasphemy." Jesus could have avoided a painful death if He has just said to the Jewish leaders, "Aw, shucks. I was just kidding. I didn't really mean that God the Father and I are one." ***The ultimate proof that Jesus is God is that He was raised from the dead!***

The immediate followers of Jesus, the Apostles, were also convinced that Jesus was "God." Jesus came to them after He was crucified and died on the cross. He talked to them and had a meal with them. They were so convinced that Jesus Christ was Divine and there is life after death they willingly died as martyrs proclaiming the Good News that "Christ has died, Christ is Risen, and Christ will come again!"

It is important to note the historical connection between Catholicism and Judaism. Catholicism considers Judaism as Version 1 of Catholicism. Then upon the arrival of Jesus Christ on the scene, the historical roots and Divine essence of Judaism was incorporated into Catholicism Version 2. This concept is shown in Figure E which follows.

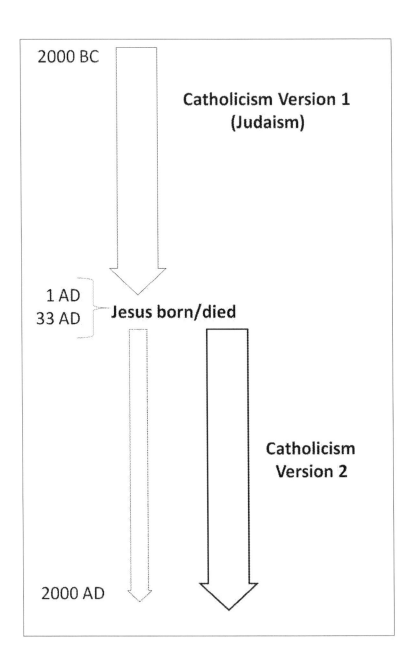

Let me get back to the main point. What does it mean to be Catholic? First of all it means that we believe that there is one God who consists of three unique persons, the Father, the Son, and the Holy Spirit, and furthermore we believe that the Father sent His son Jesus to the earth to set us "free." But what does that mean? To free us? What it means is that without Jesus Christ coming to show us "the way" to eternal happiness, we would wander blindly in the desert of life living in unhealthy ways and end up in a bad place we call Hell.

So one of the things Catholics believe is that there is a Heaven and a Hell. Which also presumes that there is life after death. Death is merely a transition to a new, more exciting, pain-free, fulfilling, creative life with our Creator, God, and with all other people who chose to go to Heaven by virtue of their decisions and actions here on earth. Hell is the place where people go who have decided to disobey the will of God and remain unrepentant in that disobedience. For those rebelling against God, their decisions and their actions result in them going to a place where there is "weeping and gnashing of teeth" (Matthew 13:42). In other words it is a bad place; it is not a good place. And more scary, we are taught that it goes on for eternity. That means there is no way out, ever. The pain never ends. The thought of that is extremely terrifying.

Let me repeat this important point. There are two kinds of actions that people take which determine whether they go to Heaven or Hell. These actions demonstrate the choice they make. The good actions or habits we call virtues; the bad actions or habits we call vices or sin. An example of a good action is giving food to a hungry person who has no money. An example of a sin would be stealing food from a hungry person. In the case of virtues we are habitually helping others and serving others. In the case of vices, or sins, we are habitually hurting others or our self.

Consistent with the traditional teachings of the Catholic Church, many of the Saints and mystics have seen visions of Heaven, Hell, and Purgatory. Some of the Medjugorje visionaries have had that experience. It is documented on the website www.medjugorje.com.

Also, Saint Sister Faustina describes in great detail what she saw when an Angel led her to the chasms of Hell. Her description is in her diary, Paragraph 741. Her diary has been published as a book entitled *Divine Mercy in My Soul*. I will list here some of the tortures Faustina mentions:

- loss of God
- perpetual remorse of conscience
- one's condition will never change
- spiritual fire will penetrate the soul
- continual darkness; terrible suffocating smell
- constant company of Satan
- horrible despair, hatred of God, vile words, curses, and blasphemies
- special tortures which relate to the manner in which the person has sinned

Sister Faustina says, "I would have died at the very sight of these tortures if the omnipotence of God had not supported me. Let the sinner know that he will be tortured throughout all eternity, in those senses which he made use of to sin. I am writing this at the command of God, so that no soul may find an excuse by saying there is no Hell, or that nobody has ever been there, and so no one can say what it is like." Sister Faustina goes on to say, "I noticed one thing about Hell. *Most of the souls there are those who disbelieve that there is a Hell.*"

A key Catholic teaching must be noted here. God predestines no one to go to Hell. At our *Last Judgment*, the truth of each person's *relationship with God* will be laid bare in the presence of Jesus Christ, who is Truth itself. Then Jesus will separate each person into one of *two groups* based on their relationship with God: *the righteous and the damned*. The righteous group will go to eternal life, which is Heaven. The unrepentant sinners, the damned, will go away to eternal punishment, which is Hell (see Matthew 25:31-46).

So what is my urgent advice? *Meditate on your relationship with God!* To be righteous is to be "right" with God: to be obedient to His will. When you sin, be repentant! Reconcile via a Sacramental Confession!

Finally, all the essential principles of the Catholic Church are included in a prayer we refer to as "the Creed." The earliest version of this was called the **Apostle's Creed**. A more refined version, called the **Nicene Creed**, is normally used to declare the basic teachings of the Catholic Church. The Nicene Creed is included in Appendix V.

The Authority of the Pope and Bishops (Magisterium)

As Catholics, we have literally thousands of people who we could call our "headquarters staff," whose full-time job is to try to understand what Jesus said, what Jesus meant, and how that should be translated into our daily lives and actions. ***Thus, to be Catholic means to accept the Bible and to accept the authority of the Catholic Bishops to determine the proper interpretation of the Bible in our day and age. As mentioned earlier, that interpretation is documented in the book we refer to as The Catechism of the Catholic Church.***

The latest version of the Catholic Catechism was published in the year 1992. The previous version, the Baltimore Catechism, was made available in the year 1853. The newest catechism addresses issues such as marriage, abortion, birth control, and homosexuality which are hot topics in this day and age. It also includes information about traditional teachings such as prayer, worship, chastity, and social justice.

The Catechism of the Catholic Church

The most important document with respect to the teachings of the Catholic Church is the <u>Bible</u>. The second most important document is the <u>Catechism of the Catholic Church</u>.

The Catechism is one book about 800 pages in length which explains the teachings of the Catholic Church. Every Catholic should have a copy of this book.

The book has four major sections:

- **Catechism Part One** explains what we believe. The summary of what we believe is contained in the prayer called the Nicene

Creed. See Appendix V for this prayer. Note that this prayer evolved from the Apostle Creed. This prayer is said during every Sunday Mass.

- **Catechism Part Two** explains how we celebrate our Christian faith with the *Eucharistic Liturgy*, also known as the *Mass*, and the *seven Sacraments* of the Church. The seven Sacraments are as follows: Baptism, Confirmation, Eucharist (or Communion), Penance or Reconciliation (or Confession), Anointing of the Sick, Holy Orders (priesthood), and Matrimony (marriage).
- **Catechism Part Three** explains how we can live our life in Christ. It covers *morality* in the context of the *Ten Commandments* and the *Natural Moral Law*.
- **Catechism Part Four** addresses Christian prayer. *The Lord's Prayer, also known as the "Our Father," is covered in detail.* Also other forms of prayer and the basic approach to prayer is covered in this section.

The current version of the Catechism of the Catholic Church was given to the world in 1992 by Pope John Paul II. In signing this document he refers to himself as the Servant of the Servants of God. Thus the Catholic Bishops are called the Servants of God; and Pope John Paul II refers to himself as the Servant of the Bishops.

The teachings within the Catholic Catechism are crucial to our understanding of the faith and need to be understood. These teachings provided me with key portions of the framework for the <u>*urgent advice*</u> *I give you.*

Appendix V. The Nicene Creed

I believe in one God, the Father Almighty, maker of heaven and earth, of all things visible and invisible.

I believe in one Lord, Jesus Christ, the Only Begotten Son of God, born of the Father before all ages. God from God, Light from Light, true God from true God, begotten, not made, consubstantial with the Father; through him all things were made. For us men and our salvation he came down from heaven, and by the Holy Spirit was incarnate of the **Virgin Mary**, and became man. For our sake he was crucified under Pontius Pilate, he suffered death and was buried, and rose again on the third day in accordance with the Scriptures. He ascended into heaven and is seated at the right hand of the Father. He will come again in glory to judge the living and the dead and his kingdom will have no end.

I believe in the Holy Spirit, the Lord, the giver of life, who proceeds from the Father and the Son, who with the Father and the Son is adored and glorified, who has spoken through the prophets.

I believe in one, holy, catholic and apostolic Church. I confess one Baptism for the forgiveness of sins and I look forward to the resurrection of the dead and the life of the world to come.

Amen.

Appendix VI. The Ten Commandments

1. I am the Lord your God: you shall not have strange gods before me.
2. You shall not take the name of the Lord your God in vain.
3. Remember to keep holy the Lord's Day.
4. Honor your father and your mother.
5. You shall not kill.
6. You shall not commit adultery.
7. You shall not steal.
8. You shall not bear false witness against your neighbor.
9. You shall not covet your neighbor's spouse.
10. You shall not covet your neighbor's goods.

Appendix VII. The Rosary Meditations

I have included here the meditations I use for each decade of the Rosary. A version of these meditations were in a pamphlet called "Pray the Rosary Daily" that is distributed by the Association of Marian Helpers (www.marian.org).

Meditate - Joyful Mysteries	Meditate on These Virtues
The Annunciation	Humility
The Visitation	Love of neighbor
The Birth of Jesus	Poverty
The Presentation in the Temple	Obedience
Finding of Jesus in the Temple	Piety

Meditate - Sorrowful Mysteries	Meditate on These Virtues
The Agony in the Garden	True sorrow for our sins
The Scourging at the Pillar	Purity
The Crowning of Thorns	Moral courage
The Carrying of the Cross	Patience
The Crucifixion	Perseverance

Meditate - Glorious Mysteries	Meditate on These Virtues
The Resurrection	Faith
The Ascension of Jesus	Hope
The Descent of the Holy Spirit	Love of God
The Assumption of Mary	Grace of a happy death
The Coronation of Mary	Trust in Mary's intercession

Meditate - Luminous Mysteries	Meditate on These Virtues
The Baptism of Jesus	Openness to the Holy Spirit
The Wedding at Cana	To Jesus through Mary
Proclaiming the Kingdom	Repentance and trust in God
The Transfiguration	Desire for holiness
The Institution of the Eucharist	Increased adoration

About The Author

Robert A. Young, also known as Grandpa Bob Young, currently lives in Connecticut with Mary, his wife of fifty years. They have nine children (*eight of whom are married*) and twenty-nine grandchildren (*so far*).

Bob and Mary are avid Christians. Their spiritual views are consistent with the teachings of the Catholic Church. Their goal is to practice their faith to the best of their ability and listen to the voice of God and obey. But of course they acknowledge their sinfulness and understand the nature of temptation. They appreciate the on-going need for forgiveness and reconciliation.

More information about the Young family can be found on their website at www.calltobefree.com.